Collaborative
Teacher
Leadership

Collaborative Teacher Leadership

How Teachers Can Foster Equitable Schools

Martin L. Krovetz   Gilberto Arriaza

CORWIN PRESS
A SAGE Publications Company
Thousand Oaks, California

For information:

Corwin Press
A Sage Publications Company
2455 Teller Road
Thousand Oaks, California 91320
www.corwinpress.com

Sage Publications Ltd.
1 Oliver's Yard
55 City Road
London EC1Y 1SP
United Kingdom

Sage Publications India Pvt. Ltd.
B-42, Panchsheel Enclave
Post Box 4109
New Delhi 110 017 India

Printed in the United States of America.

Library of Congress Cataloging-in-Publication Data

Krovetz, Martin L.
Collaborative teacher leadership: How teachers can foster equitable schools / Martin L. Krovetz, Gilberto Arriaza.
    p. cm.
Includes bibliographical references and index.
ISBN 1-4129-0501-X (cloth) — ISBN 1-4129-0502-8 (pbk.)
    1. Teacher participation in administration. 2. Teacher effectiveness. 3. Educational leadership. 4. School management and organization. I. Arriaza, Gilberto. II. Title.
LB2806.45.K76 2006
371.1'06—dc22   2005032722

This book is printed on acid-free paper.

06   07   08   09   10   9   8   7   6   5   4   3   2   1

Acquisitions Editor:	Rachel Livsey
Editorial Assistant:	Phyllis Cappello
Production Editor:	Diane S. Foster
Copy Editor:	Robert Holm
Typesetter:	C&M Digitals (P) Ltd.
Proofreader:	Maria Alonzo
Indexer:	Kathy Paparchontis
Cover Designer:	Rose Storey

Contents

Preface

In the fall of 1996, I (Marty Krovetz) held a series of focus group meetings in two school districts in our region, talking with more than 100 teachers from the Oak Grove and Campbell School Districts about what they might want as a focus for a collaborative master's program that partnered the College of Education at San Jose State University (SJSU) with their districts. I had anticipated that they would say literacy or instructional technology, and I would have worked with the appropriate faculty at SJSU to develop such a program. However, teachers said to me,

> We are being asked to play increasingly important leadership roles in our schools and districts, and we are flying by the seats of our pants. We want to participate in meetings that matter. We want to be productive. *We need a master's program that focuses on teacher leadership!*

My heart pounded. My smile was impossible to conceal. They were speaking to my passion. During the 14 years I served as a high school principal, I was proud of how well I worked with and mentored teacher leaders and how well many teacher leaders had mentored me. I knew that I was not the most *powerful* person on campus, that the school secretary, head custodian, and many teachers had far more influence than I did. I believe deeply that schools cannot be successful and sustain the hard work of challenging all students to use their minds and hearts well unless teacher leaders work collaboratively and skillfully together and with the principal and district to this end.

Working with several members of the faculty of the College of Education at SJSU and with leaders from both Oak Grove and Campbell, we developed a curriculum and sequence of classes that we thought would help teachers become skillful teacher leaders and would be rigorous enough to meet the requirements of a master's program. In the fall of 1997, we began our first cohort with 40 teachers from the two districts. Since that time, we have graduated or currently enroll approximately 700 teachers from over 20 school districts. We named this program the Master's in Collaborative Leadership program (MACL).

In designing this program, our thinking was influenced by a book by Marilyn Katzenmeyer and Gayle Moller (1996) titled *Awakening the Sleeping Giant: Leadership Development for Teachers*. A book by Linda Lambert published in 1998 titled *Building Leadership Capacity in Schools* also influenced our thinking and curriculum design. While we loved both books, neither focused on the voices of teachers who are *awakening* and whose *capacity for leadership* are being built.

Our thinking was also influenced by the writing of Bonnie Benard (1991) on resiliency. The concept of resiliency speaks to the heart of our passion for the importance of schooling. We know that students learn best in schools where they are known well, where expectations are high and support is purposeful, and where student voices are valued. We also know that a school cannot foster resiliency for students if it does not do so for adults. This led me to write a book (1999) focused on seven schools in our region, including one in Oak Grove and one in Campbell, that I felt fostered resiliency for all students and adults. The construct of resiliency is at the heart of our work.

Four assumptions about leadership guide our thinking:

1. We define leadership in the broad sense of formal and informal leadership. In this sense, every person can be a leader.

2. It is almost impossible to improve and sustain quality schools one at a time. Coherence with district leadership is vital if the focus on student learning is to be sustained over time.

3. Improving and sustaining public schooling as a vital institution is central to strengthening our democratic society.

4. School leadership is all about maximizing the learning of every student.

Students in MACL are doing incredibly courageous leadership work at their schools and districts. While in our program, they document the impact of their leadership on student learning through their action research projects (ARP). Their exit portfolios and class writings are testimonies rich in experiences and reflection. After graduation, they continue to collaborate as teams and as individuals in addressing the most complex and difficult issues, either as the new cadre of vice principals and principals or as teacher leaders at the level of the classroom, the school as a whole, and in many cases at the district level. We thought that their stories needed to be told in their own words.

We decided to write this book with the intent to capture their struggles, their victories, their challenges. We wanted this book *not* to be *about* teacher leaders, but one written by them. Our goal was to make sure that their voices would thread a narrative capturing this kind of new, skillful, collaborative teacher leader. That is why we focused on their personal stories, hoping that these would give the reader a sense not only of what this type of leadership means but also how it feels. The task was daunting. Over one year we met with many of our graduates. First, we organized a series of consultancies with large groups of our MACL graduates, asking for their input as to themes, issues, and style. Then from these consultancies we organized an editorial board made up of eight graduates who advised and guided us on the organization of the chapters, the selection of materials, and style uniformity. Finally, Joan Martens, one of these teacher leaders, edited the drafts of chapters. Yet at the end of the day, we know that this book's authenticity hinges on the reader's final word. We certainly hope to have accomplished what we set ourselves to do: to bring to the forefront the voices of new, refreshing types of educational leaders.

It is our hope that readers will use the specific narratives, Reflective Questions, and Resources presented in this book to focus discussions on how leadership capacity can be more fully developed in your schools. The *habits of mind* that the teacher leaders write about—use of data, focus on equity, job-embedded professional development, leading and managing change, courageous followership, advocacy, and so forth—can be at the heart of the work of school leaders in any school. The university-school partnership that we are engaged in helps emerging leaders develop these habits of mind, but any school or district dedicated to building leadership capacity can focus professional development around learning and practicing such habits of mind. We know that the nature of leadership changes in schools that focus in this way. We know that accountability for student learning is the dominating theme in such schools. We hope this book inspires you to pursue this work.

ORGANIZATION OF THE BOOK

In this book, teacher voices speak in the first person. We have included several dozen essays written by the graduates of our program. We made a conscious decision not to abridge the writing so that the reader can see the fullness of their deliberations. Their voices are clear, as they passionately reflect upon the impact they are having on the culture of their schools and on the learning of their students.

We are fans of Grant Wiggins and Jay McTighe's (1998) *Understanding by Design* process. Therefore, we begin each chapter with Enduring Understandings, which are meant to be clear statements about our focus for that chapter, and end each chapter with Essential Questions that should help the reader reflect on the main points of that chapter. In between, we include Reflective Questions that we hope the reader will use to personalize the stories to your own work situation. Please use these questions to engage others in the conversation.

In Chapter 1, we argue that the nature of what it means to be a teacher changes in schools focused on building leadership capacity. We present teacher writing that explains how the nature of work becomes more focused. Furthermore, they write that the culture is more based on teacher voice, using evidence and quality job-embedded professional development. Teachers write about how the quality of life and learning improve when schools build leadership capacity. We close by introducing resiliency as a lens for reframing school culture.

In Chapter 2, we make the case that the principal-as-hero model will not lead to high student achievement that is sustainable over time and that *distributed leadership*, based on involving skillful teacher leaders, has a more powerful, long-term effect on student achievement. Teachers write about the skills, attitudes, and behaviors that they use in their schools. They write about how roles and relationships change and that teachers educate teachers, act as advocates, and use challenges to impact teacher and student learning.

In Chapter 3, we present the challenges, commitments, and struggles of teacher leaders engaged in closing the academic achievement gap. Our theory of action is that good teaching translates into maximizing learning for all students, which translates into teaching students to use their minds and hearts well. Teacher leaders tell how they have placed this principle at the center of their efforts. Equally important, they tell how they struggle to align resources with this focus in mind.

In Chapter 4, we argue that knowledge creation in schools is an important function of teachers. In order for that to happen though, we also propose some preconditions. One is the need for teachers to study their practices collaboratively. The model we propose here is *collaborative action research*. A second condition is that inquiry begins in the classroom but must be connected to the whole institution. Teacher leaders write about the human scale of cultural and systemic change in their schools and about change conceived for the long haul.

In Chapter 5, we propose the notion of *equity* as the guiding purpose of school leadership. Thus, equity must be conceived as a principle and a way of being. Teacher leaders narrate how they engage their colleagues, the administration, and their communities around achieving equitable outcomes. Everything begins with knowing all students well. Then they write about their function as agents who make principles and habits happen. Equally important, teacher leaders show the skills necessary to find out whether a school is achieving equity of opportunity and outcomes.

In Chapter 6, we demonstrate that students are most successful in school when school leaders serve as *advocates* and involve the school's staff, parents, and general community in the education of all children. Teachers write about advocating for special needs students and the whole child. They write about engaging parents as advocates for student learning and about advocating for beginning teachers, for quality professional development, and for equitable working conditions. We also present writing about a situation when teachers became involved politically in local school issues.

In Chapter 7, teachers write about how changing school culture in order to better maximize learning for all students necessitates leaders skilled in *leading and managing both change and transition*. Furthermore, they write about how courageous followership is required to improve the quality of learning in a school. Teachers write about lessons learned through their failures as well as their successes.

APPLYING THE CONCEPTS IN YOUR WORKPLACE

We recognize that most of you will not have a university-school partnership to support your work. At the end of each chapter, we include reflections on how you, as a school leader(s), could use that chapter to build leadership capacity at your work site. It is our sincere hope that leadership teams will use specific teacher narratives and Reflective and Essential Questions for collaborative reflection and build the leadership capacity at your workplace. Everything begins with knowing all students well. We know that students learn best in schools where leadership capacity is strong. Two quotes bring this home:

> We need to create more opportunities for vigorous, substantive leadership, to more fully develop and capitalize on teachers' expertise without forcing them to leave the classroom. The combination of an administrator and a practicing teacher is a powerful one—able to bring both authority and classroom credibility together in the service of results. (Schmoker, 2001, p. 128)

> Most educators are concerned with their legacies: We don't want to look over our shoulders at a school we left three years ago to find that the improvements we've helped introduce have been reversed or neglected. Luckily, it is possible to develop the leadership capacity in schools and districts so that improvements remain, adults keep learning, student performance continues to advance. Leadership capacity offers us the promise of sustainable school improvement by:
> - Developing formal leaders as thoughtful, focused, and collaborative instructional leaders;
> - Turning all adults within the school community—teachers, staff, parents, and community members—into reflective, skillful coleaders;
> - Achieving steady and lasting improvement in student performance and development; and
> - Constructing schools and districts that are sustainable learning organizations. (Lambert, 2003a, p. x)

A WORD FROM THE AUTHORS

As we reviewed and discussed the writing of the teachers who contributed to this book, we recognized the diversity of their voices. We also recognized the different voices in our own writing styles. One of the beauties of this book, we hope, is that the reader will appreciate the wide range of voices presented. These voices originate from our multiple experiences, as we embrace our gender, linguistic, socioeconomic, professional, formal education and training, and geographical origins, but with profound warmth and respect.

Acknowledgments

Working with teachers who accept the challenge to become skillful, courageous school leaders is exciting. Watching them focus a school community on improving the learning of all students is inspirational. This book is a testimonial to their professionalism.

In particular, we want to thank those former students who served as our editorial board: Joan Martens, Mary Beth Boyle, Sally Peck, Julianne Knapp, Cori Wilson, Lisa Blanc, Barbara Friedenbach, and Kiva Qualls. We want to offer special acknowledgment to Joan Martens, who both served on the editorial board and read and commented on the full text, guiding our rewrites and attempts to bring coherence to this book.

We want to express our most profound respect and appreciation to each teacher leader whose narrative sits at the center of this book.

Many people have worked to make the Master's in Collaborative Leadership program successful. Our many K–12 partners and friends: We would not be doing this program without the enthusiasm and feedback from practitioners who understand and practice this work. In so many cases, their coteaching classes and mentoring have substantially enriched the learning of their emerging teacher leaders, our students. Support from SJSU Dean Susan Meyers and SJSU faculty Mary Male, Andrea Whitaker, and Nancy Markowitz was instrumental in developing this program. We are lucky to work with a wonderful group of colleagues in our Educational Leadership Department: Phyllis Lindstrom, Noni

Reis, Jim Ritchie, Gerry Chartrand, Pat Stelwagon, Steve Fiss, Barbara Gottesman, and particularly Marsha Speck, whose leadership with the Urban High School Leadership Program, books on professional development, and friendship are so integral to our work.

We are thankful to authors who influence our thinking about teacher leadership: Linda Lambert, Ann Lieberman, Bonnie Benard, Emmy Werner, Roland Barth, Michael Fullan, Andy Hargreaves, Marilyn Katzenmeyer, Gayle Moller, Deborah Meier, Grant Wiggins, Jay McTighe, William Bridges, and Ira Chaleff.

We thank the Hewlett Foundation and Ray Bachetti for the initial funding to start MACL.

We thank Rachel Livsey, our editor at Corwin, for her support and trust.

And finally, we thank our families for tolerating the hours we spent in our offices working on this manuscript.

The contributions of the following reviewers are gratefully acknowledged:

Patricia Schwartz
Principal
Thomas Jefferson Middle School
Teaneck, NJ

Mike Greenwood
Teacher leader
Windsor Public Schools
Windsor, CT

Frank Crowther
Dean of Education and Pro-Vice Chancellor
Regional Engagement and Social Justice
University of Queensland
Toowoomba, Queensland, Australia

Acknowledgments

Pam Hankins
Staff Development Specialist
Springfield Public Schools
Springfield, MO

Ellen Berg
Eighth Grade English and History Teacher
San Diego Cooperative Charter School
San Diego, CA

About the Authors

Gilberto Arriaza received his PhD from the University of California at Berkeley in the year 2000 and is an Associate Professor of Educational Leadership at San Jose State University and the Codirector of the LEAD Center, a regional center of the Coalition of Essential Schools. He has worked as advisor for school principals and leaders from K–12 schools in the larger Bay Area, has published extensively, and presented in numerous conferences on issues ranging from organizational culture, identity, leadership, and action research to discourse and language. He can be reached at One Washington Square, San Jose, CA 95192–0072, or via e-mail at garriaza@email.sjsu.edu

Martin L. Krovetz is a Professor of Educational Leadership at San Jose State University and the Codirector of the LEAD Center, a regional center of the Coalition of Essential Schools. From 1977 to 1991, he was a high school principal. He has published numerous articles on leading and managing change and is the author of *Fostering Resiliency: Expecting All Students to Use Their Minds and Hearts Well*, published by Corwin Press in 1999. He has presented at many national conferences, including ASCD, AERA, and the

Coalition of Essential Schools' Fall Forum. He received his BA from the University of Florida and his PhD from the University of North Carolina. He can be reached at One Washington Square, San Jose, CA 95192–0072 or via e-mail at mkrovetz@email .sjsu.edu

CHAPTER ONE

Reframing School Culture

Enduring Understanding

- The nature of what it means to be a teacher changes in schools focusing on building leadership capacity.

Organizations that will truly excel in the future will be the organizations that discover how to tap people's commitment and capacity to learn at all levels in an organization.

(Senge, 2000, p. 14)

Capacity-building principals align their actions to the belief that everyone has the right, responsibility and capability to work as a leader.

(Lambert, 2003a, p. 43)

S chools that excel typically have capacity-building principals who understand that sharing leadership for teaching and learning improves the quality of student learning and increases their own influence as school leaders as well. Such principals empower teachers, who then see themselves as leaders with influence both within their classrooms and throughout the school. Such schools typically work with district administrators who model and create conditions that foster skillful collaborative leadership. When these conditions are in place, everyone discovers the potential to positively influence student learning through collaborative actions. As Senge and Lambert allude to on page 1, schools and school districts that truly excel focus on learning of all students *and* all adults. In other words, transformative leaders facilitate this kind of community of practice.

In many schools, the principal is seen in a parent role, the mother or father figure, whose job it is to take care of teachers, who then should take care of students. A principal in this kind of role too often tries to be all things to all people, *a hero.* Even when that principal is collaborative in nature, teachers seldom see themselves as responsible for student and adult learning outside of their own classrooms. The culture of schooling needs to be reframed in such a way that all adults accept responsibility for the learning of all children and their own peers. This book is about teachers and administrators who are accepting this responsibility.

> What is needed is a new kind of leadership, principals who are willing to commit to leading for student accomplishment, for organizational health, for professional learning, and for long-range and deep improvements. These leaders work seriously to support the transformation of schooling and teaching and understand the importance of helping to build a learning community that includes all teachers and students. These are not "lone rangers" who depend on charisma and individual genius to transform schools. Rather, they are collaborative learners and teachers who

advocate for democratic principles. They work diligently with their faculty and their community to make bold visions a reality (p. 40). . . . Principals and teachers in schools that are in the midst of change are finding that as they do their work, they are blurring boundaries and forging new connections between leading, learning and teaching. Their schools are leadership dense organizations. (Lieberman & Miller, 1999, p. 46)

In *leadership dense* school districts and schools, certain conditions are present (based on Katzenmeyer & Moller, 1996, 2001):

1. All teachers are expected to engage in leadership activities.

2. Leadership includes both the formal and informal functions that occur within a school.

3. Assuming leadership functions does not require that one leave the classroom.

4. The primary focus of teacher leadership is teaching and learning, focused on the learning of all students and adults.

5. Teachers have the time to be reflective practitioners who solve problems around teaching and learning.

6. Professional development is job embedded, long-term, planned, purposeful, differentiated, and systematic.

7. Teacher leaders accept both the opportunities and responsibilities that come with leadership. Teacher leaders hold themselves accountable for student learning.

Building leadership impacts student learning! Research, as reported in Lambert (2003a), supports a direct connection between forging leadership capacity and student achievement:

- Conzemius and O'Neill (2001) report that when there is a shared responsibility for student learning, every ethnic subgroup improves in academic performance.
- Reeves (2000) contends that the success of the 90/90/90[1] schools is tied to school practice in which teachers are involved in improving practice together within a professional culture.
- Lewis (2002) writes that in schools in which teachers had created strong professional communities with frequent teacher collaboration, reflective dialogue, and shared norms, students were four times more likely to improve academically than in schools with weaker professional communities.

This commonsense finding is reported also by Waters, Marzano, and McNulty (2003) in their meta-analysis of 30 years of research on the effect of leadership on student achievement.

In this chapter, we introduce teacher voices to describe how the lives and work of teachers change in schools focusing on building leadership capacity. Note how the seven conditions listed above are reflected in the teacher writings throughout this chapter.

WHAT I AM BECOMING

The following was written by Elidia Boddie, an elementary school teacher leader:

> Now I feel that our team has changed from meteors to a united cluster of comets that, after they shine, leave tails of change.

When leadership capacity is fostered, teachers reflect on how they view themselves as teachers and leaders. Linda Lambert writes:

A teacher leader may be seen as a person in whom the dream of making a difference has been kept alive, or has been reawakened, by engaging colleagues in a true community of practice. Those who have managed to keep their sense of purpose alive and well are reflective, inquisitive, focused on improving their craft, action oriented; they accept responsibility for student learning and have a strong sense of self. That is, they know themselves and their intentions enough so that they are not intimidated into silence by others. When the source of reawakening is outside the school, these individuals may not be able to stay long in their own schools. (2003b, p. 3)

Amy Vanderbosch's and Jennifer Schmidt's reflections exemplify this reawakening.

Amy writes:

It is the compelling passion for my school that has forced me to overcome some of the obstacles I faced as I embarked upon this journey to become a school leader. My fear of standing up for my ideals to those with clout has not dissolved. Instead, the need to speak up for my ideals has become more important than the risks. I have a responsibility to articulate those ideals that are most important for student learning until I am heard. Across the board, in talking about data, collaboration, and communication, the understanding that I have an obligation to lead with credibility, and teach and collaborate with my colleagues, bolsters me constantly. My passion and concerns are not going unheard as in the past.

Jennifer writes:

My willingness to accept leadership roles has been parallel to that of a basketball player's experience with her team and the game, from being introduced to the pastime during required physical education classes, to watching and studying the sport as a fan, then finally joining the varsity team and courageously following the coach. At first, I was not even interested in watching. I started out in the teaching profession as many other teachers do, overwhelmed with classroom management, grading papers, and developing my teaching repertoire. The first high school I taught at was fairly large at 2,000 students and over 100 teachers. Being new to the profession and only 22, I had no clue that teachers did anything other than teach. I honestly thought the principal was there to hire, fire, and keep order at the school. Every once in a while I would be assigned to committees, and I was really confused about what we were trying to accomplish. I went to the game only if it was required. I came, dressed out, even attempted to play, but was never a team captain and was often picked last because of poor skills and understanding, which was fine with me. Can't I just teach? Not only did I not want to watch the "game," I did not even know it existed. I had not even begun to grow as a leader.

I entered the master's program during my seventh year as a teacher. In the first year of the program, I was steeped in learning about superstar players and their own approaches to the game. Deborah Meier and Linda Darling-Hammond were best at this teacher leadership challenge, and reading their writing helped me reflect on what is worth fighting for. I learned about leadership by watching the professors, the other students in class, and my own team. Although I often felt like a spectator, I was becoming more of a leader in shaping my own department. Afflicted with acute shyness in large settings, I found that the Math Department was just the right size to try out my emerging leadership skills.

Our Math Department was told that we needed to drop one of our courses for the next year. We had a very successful calculus program with both AB and BC courses structured as yearlong classes, which unfortunately took up many of our allotted sections. As a department, we devised a plan to make the AB course a semester long class, rather than drop it entirely. I taught the Calculus AB class and felt a strong connection to its success and was proud of the students' achievements. When it seemed the Math Department was blindsided by the administration's decision to completely cancel Calculus AB, the group chose me to talk with our principal and assistant principal to discuss alternatives. I would have never done this before my participation in the leadership program—maybe simmered and been angry, but not confronted the principal.

I went armed with ideas on how to best present my case. When it seemed those ideas would not be good enough, I felt defeated and unsupported. We had had a 100% passing rate for two years running. In the summer, I would find out that it would be three years in a row. I asked, "How did this happen? Why was no one in the Math Department asked about how to schedule the classes?" I called the administration on it. Although this sounds ridiculous to people who have never been afraid to confront authority, I was shaking inside when I asked. I found courage and strength in my belief that this issue was too important for me to back down.

My struggles now are between wanting to be on the team to play varsity but feeling warm and comfortable on the bench. As we all know, leadership is not a spectator sport. I still struggle to feel comfortable when speaking up. Even though I struggle to make jump shots, it does not mean I should quit the game. As with all sports, practice makes perfect. I have been attempting to speak up, and my math colleagues have taken notice of this. In fact, when I asked one colleague if she had noticed any growth in me as a leader, her first comment was that I speak up more and allow myself to state my beliefs even if they challenge someone else. She said it was refreshing to see, even though I have disagreed with her a few times.

Reflective Questions

- Beyond the confines of your classroom, what are you becoming?
- What specific modeling and support are there for teachers in your workplace to develop as leaders?

WHAT DOES THIS LOOK LIKE?
CHANGING THE NATURE OF WORK

Able people—wise people—take jobs where they are entrusted with important tasks. Create a school without collegial trust and the authority to carry out improvements and you will create a third-rate school. Its faculty will be placeholders, not wise people. (Barth, 1990, p. xii)

In a leadership dense school, the work of being a teacher and administrator changes:

- The school community is more clearly focused on maximizing learning for *all* students.
- School leaders experience having a significant voice over the workings of the school, know their voices are valued, and more actively listen to the voices of colleagues, parents, and students.
- School leaders create a culture of evidence based on regular collection, analysis, and use of data to improve instructional practice.
- Leadership capacity is fostered as a result of job-embedded, high-quality, professional development that leads to growth as a teacher and as a leader.
- School leaders improve the quality of life and learning for adults and students at school and in the district.

Crowther, Kaagan, Ferguson, and Hann (2002) write about parallel leadership. They argue that if schools are going to transform teaching and learning, a relationship must exist between teacher leaders and administration that builds the knowledge-generating capacity of schools. The collective action of teachers and administrators should be built on mutual respect, shared purpose, and allowance for individual expression.

As the teacher leaders write in each of the sections below, life is not the same when you become aware of the impact your actions have on the learning of students and adults throughout the school. You can understand that how they view their work has changed and that students will benefit.

Kristin Pfotenhauer-Sharp writes about the importance of focused staff collaboration. A letter from a middle school team of teacher leaders to their new principal demonstrates the courage that comes with expecting your voices to matter.

Facilitating professional development for a number of years now, I have often been frustrated with the lack of focus. The principals I have worked with have often relied on the "tyranny of the urgency" that is on addressing pressing issues with little or no regard for the long-range needs of improving teaching and learning. So although my organization and facilitation skills have improved, it has never been very satisfying. Working with the current school leadership team and the Action Research Team and chairing the Western Association of Schools and Colleges (WASC) accreditation process is enabling me to support a focused staff development plan.

Part of the WASC process involves developing an action plan for the next three to six years. I recently designed and facilitated the meetings that produced the draft of this plan.

The school staff looked at data, determined critical academic needs, and evaluated our program in relation to the WASC criteria. This was done in five interdepartmental focus areas: vision, culture, and leadership; assessment and accountability; curriculum paths; powerful teaching and learning; and student support. Then departments shared the strengths and growth needs from each area and came to consensus on three to five of these growth needs. Evening meetings were held with parents in which they read the focus group drafts, added their input, and brainstormed their own list of growth needs. A student retreat was also held. Students looked at data and shared the strengths and weaknesses, used a "big paper/chat room" activity to write their ideas to the WASC criteria, and brainstormed their list of growth needs.

Overall, I felt good about the end result. What I liked best was that we were able to include a community feedback loop with our families of English Language Learning (ELL) students.

Reflective Questions

- What is the vision for schooling in your district and school?
- How does this vision drive practice in your district and school?

The following letter to their new principal was written by Liv Barnes, Katie Dequine, Kerstin Ericsson, Kathleen McCowan Sandidge, Peter Stapes, and Amy Vanderbosch. A much beloved principal had recently left, and a new principal was assigned. The school was designated "Program Improvement" due to low test scores. A group of teachers were leading a staff effort to improve student learning and to raise those scores. The new principal had questioned their strategies for doing so. The team talked at length about how to work constructively with the principal. They hoped that, if they spoke up as a team, he would respond in a positive manner, which he in fact did.

September 25

Dear Bob, [not his real name]

We are hoping to use this letter to address some recent concerns of the team. While we recognize the extraordinary pressure that you and we are facing in light of our Program Improvement (PI) designation, we are uneasy about the redirection of our Leadership Team's focus.

The members of our Leadership Team represent all facets of our staff and have spent many hours creating a mission and objectives. We have concentrated our efforts and meeting time on enhancing our school culture. We know that school culture has a great impact on student learning. At this point, the team is ironing out details for an improved and unified discipline plan, a system for peer coaching, and greater attention to our target student population. All three of these areas directly impact instruction in the classroom and therefore student achievement. It has always been the intent that the Leadership Team address problems that the staff feels are important. It is our hope that we work together as school leaders to solve those problems.

We feel a push to address the implications of our school being labeled Program Improvement. Our staff feels the same pressure that you do, if not more. Our professionalism is being called into question, and we must endure this PI process for years to come.

A strong school culture will improve student achievement. We feel strongly that our original course of action will help us reach our goals, as well as sustain them far into the future. It is our hope to refocus the efforts of the Leadership Team toward improved school culture in this tumultuous time. We also feel honored to be a part of rewriting the school plan and hope to support your philosophies in this venue.

We welcome your feedback on our thoughts.

Respectfully,

Liv Barnes
Katie Dequine
Kerstin Ericsson
Kathleen McCowan
Peter Stapes
Amy Vanderbosch

Reflective Questions

- Whose voices are valued in your workplace? What impact do these voices have?
- What specific evidence do you have that your voice is valued in your workplace?
- How do you use your voice in your school and/or district?

The following was written by Christina Filios, Fawn Myers, and Theresa Sage about the impact teacher leaders can have when they help create a culture of evidence at their school.

Over the last semester, we learned about Schmoker's suggestions for becoming a leader with vision. Schmoker (2001) emphasized the importance of having staff work with student data to develop a vision and action plan. As we looked at our school data, our team confirmed the existence of a large achievement gap between White and Hispanic students. We decided to make this the focus of our action research project (ARP), and we challenged ourselves to present this data to our staffs. Fawn and Theresa planned a staff meeting during which they used data to help guide their colleagues' thinking about restructuring at the middle school. Christina analyzed graduation rates, drop-out rates, and test results with the

School Site Council, helping to expose parents and students to the numbers as well.

As we've developed as teacher leaders and a team, our work on our action research has acted as a springboard to effect changes at our schools and the district. Our initial data collection revealed the achievement gap, which led us to research the efficacy of our programs for English Language Learner I, II, and III students. Since our ARP was focused on such a specific population, we found ourselves broadening our vision for equity to a larger district scope.

It is imperative that school leaders use student and other relevant data to guide and improve practices around teaching and learning. Chapter 4 focuses on the impact inquiry can have on a school's culture and on student learning.

Reflective Questions

- In what ways are teachers actively engaged in data collection, analysis, reflection, and implementation at your workplace?
- What evidence do you have for the impact of this engagement?

Professional Growth

This continuing dialogue, face to face, over and over, is a powerful educative force. It is our primary form of staff development. When people ask me how we "'train'" new teachers, I say that the school itself is an educator for the kids and staff; it's its own staff development project. (Meier, 1995, p. 109)

The following was written by Robert Hatcher after reading Deborah Meier's book *Power of Their Ideas* (1995). Robert reflected that when staff conversation is about evidence, cause and effect, hypothesizing, reflection, and passion, it crosses curriculum barriers. It encourages richer conversations that overlap subject-specific ones. Using habits of mind as a general structure of a school shifts the focus to thinking about the greater world of ideas. Then he wrote the following specific example. [Teacher names have been changed.]

As part of our action research project, I presented several literacy strategies to a cross-disciplinary group of teachers. Paula, the physical science teacher, with many English Language Learning (ELL) students in her classes, said that long ago she had used the KWL strategy (what we KNOW, what we WANT to know, what we LEARNED). Minh, in the Math Department, remembered it from SDAII training, but was skeptical about its use in mathematics. Paula explained how she used the KWL at the opening of a new chapter. She said it was difficult to get students to generate the "what we know" and the "want to know" lists so she had abandoned its use. Mary, from the English Department, said she found that her ELL students were more likely to participate when they could use the book for support in generating ideas.

I encouraged them to talk about ways that this strategy might be useful. Minh suggested table groups of four as a method for developing the "what we know" list. Paula then said that the groups could open their books, search through the chapter, and make a list of what they wanted to learn. Minh suggested that, for the sake of time, each group could list five things to learn. Paula agreed and said she would have her groups rank their top three ideas. Paula suggested a short action research project on the use of KWL tracking the ELL and at-risk student participation.

At our next meeting, these teachers shared their efforts to date. In algebra classes, Minh found the KWL activity highly successful in getting his students to feel more connected to the content about to be studied. Paula reported more students expressing interest in learning about the new topics. She was pleased to see table groups claim ownership of the ideas as they were studied during the following week. Mary talked about how she had spent time in class asking students to reflect in small groups on what they had learned and paid close attention to how her ELL students approached this. During the third meeting, Paula and Minh discussed how to fine-tune the KWL activity for the next chapter.

This renewed interest in a literacy strategy brought together four teachers, including me, from different content areas in conversations focused on increasing student engagement and learning. It led to informal evidence gathering and a focus on effective strategies for at-risk students. It is clear that these teachers have developed a new cross-disciplinary relationship. What will sustain the teacher interest and pursuit of such work is now dependent upon leadership, the maintenance of the focus that has begun, and the allocation of that precious resource, time.

Reflective Questions

- What evidence do you have that the professional development plan at your workplace has a positive impact on teacher and student learning?
- In what ways has previous professional development been built upon over time?

WHY DO IT? IT IS ABOUT QUALITY OF LIFE AND LEARNING!

I think that the problem of how to change things from "I" to "we," of how to bring a good measure of collegiality and relatedness to adults who work in schools, is one that belongs on the national agenda of school improvement—at the top. It belongs at the top because the relationships amongst adults in schools are the basis, the precondition, the *sine qua non* that allow, energize, and sustain all other attempts at school improvement. Unless adults talk with one another, and help one another, very little will change. (Barth, 1990, p. 32)

Teachers ask, "What's in it for me?" "Why should I want to work in a school that builds my leadership capacity?" "Why can't I just be left alone to teach in my classroom?" The answer is that in such schools teachers experience trust, respect, intellectual stimulation, and increased job satisfaction; they feel more professional. Fawn Myers writes about how she has learned to be more in charge of her work life.

The best metaphor I can think of to describe my growth as a leader is jack-in-the-box. I liken this to the tightly coiled toy figure of the jack-in-the-box being wound by external forces and finally springing into action: Voila! An energetic teacher leader! External requests by my leaders would wind me up, and I would leap up for a new challenge. Because of personal life circumstances such as the adoption of a child, the bearing of three more children, and the increasing demands of rearing my growing brood, at times I would pull myself back into the box and close the lid.

By spring of my first year at Britton (my sixteenth year of teaching), I was invited to be part of a brainstorming team to establish a new structure for our English Language Learners. I agreed to be part of the team and volunteered to teach within the new structure. At this point, I was fully aware that I had sprung from the box, but the decision was a conscious one on my part. I began teaching within this new structure in the fall of 2002, the same semester I began the MA program. Our team was asked to gather data about our site. Theresa and I chose to present the data to our whole staff, demonstrating an achievement gap between our White and Hispanic students. I grew as a result of the process of gathering data, analyzing it, and establishing norms for discussing it. I felt empowered. For the first time professionally, I did not feel that the crank was being wound by an external leader. I was in charge in choosing when to leap and in what direction.

The following was written by Joan Gotterba:

The 2003 Fall Forum of the Coalition of Essential Schools had just been brought to a close with a thought-provoking discussion between Deborah Meier and Linda Darling-Hammond. The sounds of their voices and the significance of their ideas replayed in my mind as our group squeezed into the hotel elevator. A young man looked at us and wondered out loud who would be the next leaders to carry on the mission of sustainable change in our schools. Who indeed, I thought, for if not us, then who?

I came to the Fall Forum to help facilitate two sessions, one called "Understanding by Design" and the other "Teacher Leadership: Stories from the Heart," and to listen to speeches, discussions, and presentations. Since my return to Peterson Middle School, I have told the story of my experiences and thoughts to my family, my master's team, the master's cohort, my students, to colleagues informally at a Math Department meeting, at a faculty meeting of over 70 teachers and administrative staff, and at a district meeting of math teachers from all three Santa Clara Unified School District middle schools. In listening to the discussions that followed, I know that I am impacting the shape of things to come.

In order for sustainable change to occur in a school, a systematic approach, rather than a piecemeal one, needs to be taken. In listening to the discussions that have followed my story, this seems to be the part that scares people the most. Some who see the need for change caution against doing too much too fast. To this, I point out that we are changing already. We are experiencing:

- A new administrative team
- An imminent remodel due to earthquake retrofitting
- Ongoing task force and staff meetings to craft new vision and mission statements
- District performance-based assessments in English, science, and math
- Growing movements of Critical Friends and Backwards Design
- Five teachers in the Master's in Collaborative Leadership program at San Jose State University understanding the need for change
- Teachers attending conferences, such as five who just returned from a National Middle School Association conference in Atlanta, who are also telling their stories for change

We are in a period of *transition,* and I find the chances for change invigorating. Instead of taking a backseat, as I might have in the beginning of my career, I find myself involved in more activities than I ever thought possible to help guide the school in improving learning, teaching, and assessment. While I was in my twenties, I recall thinking that I would have absolutely no impact on decisions; it was a waste of time to even try. I now find myself Math Department chair, a mentor for Backwards Design, a member of the principal's task force for creating a new vision statement, a member of a district committee for reviewing district math standards and writing enduring understandings based on the standards, and a teacher leader working with my team on our action research. I have become more of a risk taker as I have become more knowledgeable.

The story that I have told my colleagues starts with looking at a map of our school. "What we have now is a sixth grade school and a junior high. What we could have are villages that do not need to be the same." At this point in my story, I could see two reactions on the faces of my colleagues. Some considered the possibilities while others formed the word *but* and half-raised their hands. I continued by asking, "What are we the most proud of at Peterson?"

I told my story to my students and had them write and draw what the perfect middle school would look like to them. Many wrote of the frustration of surviving in an environment that is crowded with over 1,300 students. I talked to several teachers who are often resisters. They told me the ideas are great, but that it would be an incredible amount of work. I am thrilled that I was able to start the conversations.

In response to my story, the Math Department spent time at the last meeting talking about things that we can do right away to help all students feel like they belong and can be successful. They decided to organize quarterly meetings of teachers who share common prep periods. The goal would be first to become acquainted (in a school of our size, we still don't know each other well) and then to plan activities for students. Instead of complaining that we have little common planning time, the math teachers decided to reach out across disciplines and grade levels.

Presenting at the Fall Forum[2] seemed like it would be the capstone of my Master's in Teacher Leadership experience. I realize now that it was the gateway to the next phase. It gave me a story to share. My story encompasses my experiences in life and education, as to what research shows is best for students, using data-based decision making and building a collaborative culture. I've learned by telling and reshaping the story as I listen to how others respond. My school is already changing. It needs teacher leaders to reorganize and revitalize the whole school. In gently telling my Fall Forum story, I have started the conversation.

Reflective Questions

- What opportunities exist for teachers to participate in the bigger vision of your school?
- What happens in your workplace when teachers take risks in front of and with their peers and formal leaders?
- Think of a time when teacher leaders effectively led a collaborative effort that positively impacted student learning. What did these leaders do that led to the positive result?

FOSTERING RESILIENCY:
A LENS FOR REFRAMING CULTURE

Resiliency: the ability to bounce back successfully, despite exposure to severe risks

All people want to live in and work in communities that nurture them. These places are, as in the theme song from the television program *Cheers,* places where "people know my name." Based on research by Emily Werner and Ruth Smith (1992) and the writings of Bonnie Benard (1991) and Marty Krovetz (1999), we know that people thrive in communities that (1) know them well, (2) hold high expectations for them and support them to meet these expectations, and (3) value their meaningful participation. When schools and school districts focus time and resources on building the teaching and leadership capacity of all adults, decisions and daily practice can be based on consistently asking if what is proposed and/or what is practiced will actually address each of the three factors of resiliency for the students and adults in the school. *Collaborative Teacher Leadership* is about fostering such schools.

Barbara Friedenbach writes:

When grappling with challenging situations (e.g., Jacob, the defiant student who does not engage in learning, or Travis, who seems unable to learn to read), a resilient learning community will expect me to improve my teaching practice as I search for a solution. It will expect me, as a professional, to be able to work through the challenge. When I have difficulty doing so, a resilient community will offer support to empower me. And in the end, when I am able to grow from the experience, I will have gained many things: (1) a strategy for solving similar issues, (2) greater confidence in my own teaching abilities, and (3) satisfaction that comes from seeing myself and my students succeed.

Lisa Blanc writes:

As a school leader, parent, and teacher, my fundamental belief is that the primary purpose of schooling is to develop resilient, literate children who grow up to be healthy, caring, and responsible adults. I want *all* students to be expected to use their hearts and minds well, regardless of their diverse backgrounds and needs. Each child is an individual and cannot be passed along an assembly line and stamped with a uniform quality seal. In order for teachers and leaders to empower students to use their hearts and minds well, we must break from uniformity in teaching and stretch to teach for diversity in ways that help different kinds of learners find productive paths to knowledge as they also learn to live collaboratively together. Schools that embrace student diversity and strive for equity in education for all students build capacity and resiliency in children and adults.

Reflective Questions

- What evidence do you have that your school fosters resiliency for its students? How do you know that adults know students well, have high expectations for them, support them to meet these expectations, and value their voices?
- What evidence do you have that your school fosters resiliency for its adults? How do you know that adults know adults well, have high expectations for them, support them to meet these expectations, and value their voices?

APPLYING THE CONCEPTS IN YOUR WORKPLACE

At the end of each chapter, we include a short reflection on how you can use the ideas in this chapter to build the leadership capacity of yourself and others in your workplace.

1. Read, read, read, especially the books by Katzenmeyer and Moller (2001), Lambert (2003a), and Krovetz (1999).

2. Encourage and lead your school leadership team to use the tools in these three books to assess the culture of your school.

3. Start a teacher reflection group that focuses on reading these and other books and articles together. Establish norms and practices of trust so that participants can reflect on and share "what they are becoming."

4. Use the writings and reflective questions in this chapter to start conversations. We hope that a primary value of this book will be that groups of people will read it together and use the writing of these teachers to reflect and create opportunities to grow as leaders.

5. Discuss ways to bring more focus to the goals for the school and to professional development. Use your voice(s) to talk with others in a constructive way about making professional development high quality and job embedded.

6. Use student data to lead conversations that focus on how best to improve the quality of learning for all students.

7. Use every opportunity to build leadership capacity. Staff meetings, department meetings, and grade level meetings should focus on professional development and building leadership capacity.

ESSENTIAL QUESTIONS

1. In diagnosing your own school culture, what opportunities exist to build leadership capacity?

2. In what specific ways does this occur?

3. What evidence do you have to demonstrate positive impact on student learning?

4. How did the professional lives of the teachers whose writings are included in this chapter change as their leadership capacity was developing and as they stepped forward within their school communities?

RESOURCES

Tools

There are excellent tools to evaluate school culture in Linda Lambert's book (2003a).

Case studies of schools that are focused on fostering resiliency can be found in Marty Krovetz's book (1999).

The Healthy Kids Survey developed by WestED can be found at www.wested.org/hks

Organizations

Department of Educational Leadership in the College of Education at San Jose State University: www2.sjsu.edu/edleadership/

Coalition of Essential Schools: www.essentialschools.org

Resiliency

Search Institute: www.search-institute.org

E-mail Bonnie Benard: bbenard@wested.org

Resiliency in Action: www.resiliency.com

ENDNOTES

1. 90/90/90 means that 90% or more of the students live below the poverty line, 90% or more of the students are from minority populations, and 90% or more of the students read at or above grade level.

2. The Fall Forum is the name of the annual national conference of the Coalition of Essential Schools.

CHAPTER TWO

Learning to Lead

Enduring Understandings

- Perpetuating the principal-as-hero model will not lead to high student achievement for all students that is sustainable over time.
- The quality and impact of teacher leadership is largely dependent on the teachers' skills, attitudes, and behaviors.

Never doubt that a small group of thoughtful people could change the world. Indeed, it's the only thing that ever has.

—Margaret Mead

WHY THE NEED TO DISTRIBUTE LEADERSHIP?

Talk with any excellent principal and you will hear a tale of woe: 60+ hours per week, stress, constant multitasking, and inability to focus for any length of time on instructional leadership.

Talk with any excellent teacher about her excellent principal and you will hear a respectful conversation, albeit one that focuses on the impossibility of the principal's job and how little time the principal has to focus on student learning.

Talk with any excellent superintendent about her best principals and you will hear a conversation much like that from the teacher—a respectful conversation, but one that focuses on the impossibility of the principal's job and how little time the principal has to focus on student learning.

Talk with educators who have worked in schools that have made substantial progress in student achievement and you will hear an infinite number of sad tales about how the work was not sustained and how deserted people felt after a key leader(s) left.

As a society, we place too much faith in the ability of charismatic leaders to solve problems and improve our world. In fact, charismatic leadership does not create the long-term conditions that organizations need to excel. As Michael Fullan writes:

> Charismatic leaders inadvertently often do more harm than good because, at best, they provide episodic improvement followed by frustrated or despondent dependence. Superhuman leaders also do us another disservice: they are role models who can never be emulated by large numbers. Deep and sustained reform depends on many of us, not just on the very few who are destined to be extraordinary. (2001, pp. 1–2)

At the same time, there is wide recognition that skillful leadership is a prerequisite for improving schools and student learning. Seldom, however, can one person provide this kind of leadership (Hargreaves & Fink, 2004).

This acknowledgment has led to conversations about *distributing* leadership (Spillane, Halverson, & Diamond, 2001). The concept of distributed leadership in schools is based on the recognition that many people in a school possess leadership skills and do leadership work and that by utilizing these resources in a coherent way, schools will be more effective in educating students. As Michael Fullan writes,

> The principal with a moral imperative can help realize it only by developing leadership in others. It is the combined forces of shared leadership that make a difference. School leadership is a collective enterprise. (2003, p. xv)

What Is Distributed Leadership?

- It means finding the best path by tapping the expertise, ideas, and effort of everyone involved. This is more proactive than delegating.
- It not only encourages idea sharing; it demands it.
- Everyone is not necessarily a decision maker, but everyone has expertise.
- It is about cooperation and trust. We all share the same mission, even though we contribute to it in different ways.
- It empowers people to make their jobs more efficient, meaningful, and effective.
- Under it, everyone matters.

(Based on West Chester University, 2004)

It is not enough to delegate leadership responsibilities to others. There is a science and art to leadership. One can be taught and mentored in the science of leadership. One can be inspired to learn the art of leadership. As John Goodlad writes: "There is irresponsibility in significantly expanding teachers' authority without educating them to use it" (1990,

p. 27). And, as Michael Fullan writes, "Leaders are not born; they are nurtured" (2004, p. 196).

In this chapter, we include the voices of teacher leaders who are conscientiously building their leadership capacity. Their reflections demonstrate that this is a work in progress; building one's leadership capacity is a lifelong process. As Jackie Kawashima, writes:

> Water has been called the staff of life, but when stagnant, it is useless. My professional growth, like a river, is always on the move.

THE SKILLS, ATTITUDES, AND BEHAVIORS OF SKILLFUL TEACHER LEADERS

Katzenmeyer and Moller (2001) write that as leaders develop they answer four questions: Who am I? Where am I? How do I lead? What can I do? In addressing the first two questions, Christina Filios, Fawn Myers, and Theresa Sage write about the importance of knowing their own strengths, the strengths of the other members of their team, and respecting each others' talents.

> As a team, we have grown from simply regarding one another as friends and colleagues to working collaboratively and truly respecting one another's talents. Instead of working only to improve in our weak areas as leaders, we work also to develop each other's strengths and to use these very consciously when planning our work. Theresa is our connector. She has a strong talent in bringing different players to the table and for eliciting input from different constituencies. As a department chair and union representative, she does not hesitate to initiate difficult conversations with administration. In her role as group "taskmaster," she keeps us scheduled and working toward deadlines. Her connections to powerful players at the district level have assisted us in class assignments, such as interviews and our budget presentation.
>
> Fawn is a wonderful clarifier, someone who is able to sift through whining and complaining to get to the heart of an issue. Her logical thinking and balanced approach often keep our work

focused in the right direction. This is clearly evident in her ability to ask the team tough questions when frustrations are high: "What is your purpose for doing ____?" "What is the expected outcome?" "What change will that lead to?" are all common inquiries when the group is grappling with resistance. Her compassion also reminds us that we should be helping to develop the talents and resiliency of our colleagues, rather than criticizing them. In presenting data to the staff, Fawn stayed optimistic—that all colleagues might be moved by the information.

Christina brings a fire and passion for equity and social justice. She is learning to harness some of that passion and does most of her complaining behind closed doors with her colleagues. When her school changed its support program for English Language Learning students, her passion ignited. This was a difficult learning process, as she was forced to go beyond the comfort of the team and have a difficult conversation with the administrator in charge of the program. Throughout her action research and other situations that have occurred in the district, Christina's passion brings to the forefront issues for the team to address.

Amy Vanderbosch reflects on question 3—how she leads—as part of a narrative on what she learned from practicing meeting facilitation skills:

My instructor and mentor, Gerry Chartrand, wrote the following comment on one of my assignments, "Communication is an effort to build credibility." Misguidedly, I have worked in the completely opposite direction from this theory. I have mistakenly spent countless hours of time and energy working behind closed doors, both as a teacher and since I have stepped out of the classroom into a leadership role. I was largely under the impression that if I worked diligently (in my office, in my classroom), kept things under wraps—packaged my idea, my plan for reform, or my theory of action—and then presented it in a glamorous unveiling, I would be perceived as a professional, one who gets things done and does so without a lot of guidance or assistance. I would convey my initiative, my resourcefulness, and the power of my original thinking. That would be enough to promote myself and my brilliant ideas for students and the school.

At some point, I reflected and wrote about my experience in leading a meeting. Preparing meticulously to organize the meeting and disseminating a plan of action, I made every effort to reduce the burden on the team of teachers. According to Cindy Lakin Morley (1994), an hour of preparation is necessary for each hour of meeting time. I put in that time and so much more; however, one of the most fundamental tenets that I overlooked was to engage others for feedback. After the meeting, one of our teachers said, "I don't know why you didn't share your ideas with me first. I would have told you it was too much for us." I didn't want to hear it then, but in retrospect, it was absolutely correct. I should have taken the agenda to others and modified the meeting according to their input. I have since incorporated a system of communication that keeps stakeholders informed. I strive to share myself honestly and am learning to ask for feedback. I truly have begun communicating openly with those involved and become more transparent in my plans for improving student learning.

For their action research project, one high school team chose to study the impact of developing standards-based common assessments on student learning. In reflecting on what she learned, Lori Gaines reflects on the fourth question—what she can do:

My growth as a leader began with small steps, such as starting a structured collaboration schedule with the geometry teachers at my school. I began by seeking those who would like to work on creating a standards-based fall final exam, and I found that the original goal grew. What started out as a common final became common standards-based assessments for every unit! It was very exciting to me to see a small objective bloom. I found that facilitating these meetings was so simple. All that was required was an agenda and a goal. We also wanted to collect and organize data for each standard addressed on each unit test. While this seemed a daunting task, one particular teacher in our department made it very easy due to her wonderful ideas on how to organize the data. I have learned that one great leadership quality is to seek out those people who are gifted in areas that I am not, and this revelation brings much freedom! I see that much of leadership is just starting a process, and much of the outcome is left to those participating, with the leader simply acting as facilitator. When one person takes on a leadership role, others will assume leadership roles as well.

- What skills, attitudes, and behaviors do you have and use that demonstrate your capacity as a leader?
- What skills, attitudes, and behaviors do you observe in others that you admire and find effective?

NEW ROLES, NEW RELATIONSHIPS

When teachers step forward as emerging, skillful leaders, their relationships change with positional leaders and with peers. This requires new skills. An integral skill is to learn how to lead without institutional authority or positional power. Skillful leaders understand the importance of relationship building. In this section, we present two narratives. Katie's learning is clearly painful and powerful. The writing by the middle school teachers demonstrates risk taking and the importance of skillful mentoring and modeling as done by their principal.

For their exit portfolios, teacher leaders in our program write a "story from the heart" around a compelling issue from which they learned much more about themselves as leaders. Katie Dequine writes:

For the essential questions paper last year, I answered "no" to the question that asked if I possessed the skills of a true leader. It was at a time when I was burned out from trying to guide the leadership team at my school. What defeated me in October was embracing too many roles because I tried to lead authoritatively rather than collaboratively. I made myself in charge of scheduling meetings, creating an agenda, taking notes during the meetings, and updating everyone through e-mail.

I was wounded by some of the feedback that was given to me. The criticism was partially true, hurting me even more, and it took me out of the leadership position during the months of November and December 2003. It devastated me to let go of my role because the leadership team truly created purpose in my job. I have been teaching physical education for seven years and had lost my motivation to help guide teenagers to a healthier lifestyle. It has become redundant for me, and I ache seeing children try to survive in this day and age. My motivation was gone again. The pain and hopelessness I saw in my students' eyes was now in my eyes.

I left the leadership team for two months on the counsel of some teachers in my master's group. They saw my vision, and it did not coincide with the rest of the team's. They saw my frustration in leading, and they wanted to carry the burden for a while. They wanted teachers to feel supported and nourished. I wanted the top priority to be teachers standing up and creating immediate change within the system that is not working for our students. I did not want to hear the team's feelings or problems anymore. I wanted change!

I took the time during those two months to watch and listen, and I kept silent. I saw different leaders lead within my group, and I saw their effectiveness and some of their ineffectiveness, too. I slowly began to see where I had gone wrong, and I could see what the team was lacking and how it was gradually moving toward some kind of vision. That vision has become a lot clearer to me. I do not believe I have found all of the answers to leading, nor do I believe that I have the exact same vision as everyone on the leadership team, yet I want to step into the role of a leader again.

I will be returning to the leadership team in January, but it will be very difficult to be watching on the sidelines. Somehow I have to adapt my vision to the team's vision, and that is not an easy task. I believe I have leadership skills and passion to lead within the educational system, but I also know that I have weaknesses that need work. I lack patience, I lack empathy, and I lack the ability to express my thoughts articulately. I feel that I need these skills in order to be a more productive leader. I will do my best to learn, grow, and change myself in order to benefit our students.

Our goal is that many of our teacher leaders will take courageous stances in front of their peers. We require that they do so. Mark DeRobertis, Chris Izor, Anna Williams, and Kelly Shannon went above and beyond our expectations by championing a schoolwide initiative brought to the school by their new principal. They write:

Shelly Viramontez made the bold decision to make the precepts of "All Students Can Succeed," "No Child Left Behind," and "Closing the Achievement Gap" more than just idealistic phrases. Even though she was in her first year as Monroe's principal, she offered our school as a pilot for the implementation of Mel Levine's Schools Attuned Program.[1] Now in its second year at our school, the program, although still in its infancy, has been fully introduced to all grade levels and all teachers to the point that it is now being addressed at every grade level meeting. Shelly believes she has a quality faculty, capable of making the transition to be a major systemic reform. She decided to implement Schools Attuned as a schoolwide program to be used in classrooms, supporting struggling students to be more successful.

As a first-year principal, Shelly found the process of leading change by herself overwhelming. One significant issue concerning the reform was the lack of schoolwide acceptance from teachers. Shelly is a collaborative leader who stays focused on what is best for the students. She also places resources to be consistent with priorities for student learning. During the summer of 2002, Shelly supported 15 teachers to attend the Schools Attuned training seminar, including two of the four master's team members.

This is when our master's team was presented with our first chance to really make a difference. Shelly realized that it would be advantageous to have our action research project (ARP) focus on the schoolwide implementation of the Schools Attuned program. We would have a genuine ARP that involved systemic reform and have a real opportunity to be teacher leaders. The decision of our team to have our ARP support Shelly's reform was also the result of self-examination because we found ourselves in the forefront of the charge to make it happen. Digesting the following quote from *The Courageous Follower* made it easier to accept our new role: "Successful followers care passionately about their work and the people it serves. They have a sense of ownership, of stewardship. When followers and leaders share a passion for the work, they can be full partners in it" (Chaleff, 1995, p. 48).

That September we made an introductory presentation of our ARP at a faculty meeting. Chris and Kelly led an explanation of our involvement with the implementation of Schools Attuned, reinforcing our principal's vision. In addition, Shelly communicated her wish that teachers use grade level meetings to discuss struggling students and use Schools Attuned strategies to address how to support these students. We designed a survey to inquire about how much experience each teacher had with Schools Attuned. The survey also inquired about each teacher's commitment to use the process. Individually during the following weeks, we took the time to purposefully engage our fellow teachers in conversations about the process and the benefits for them and their students.

In October, our team made another presentation at a faculty meeting. This time Mark and Anna used role playing to model the process of discussing students with Schools Attuned strategies. Shelly's plan was to establish this process as a regular function at all grade level meetings. This constituted a complete change from what many teachers had used the grade level meetings for over the course of many years.

In November, Shelly reiterated her expectation for grade level meetings to focus on discussions of struggling students and using Schools Attuned strategies as support. She delivered a schoolwide e-mail explaining this and made it known that the master's team would be facilitating grade level meetings.

Thereafter, each of us facilitated grade level meetings, using a Schools Attuned Diagnosis Form. Each student discussion is placed into a category from the Schools Attuned spreadsheet, and strategies are matched to help with each student's trait. Teachers who share the student agree to use these strategies and, at a subsequent meeting, determine if any progress is evident.

The fact that teachers can sometimes resist change brings us back to the significant issue involving the systemic reform. As previously mentioned, teachers already had other purposes for grade level meetings. Although they respected the vision of their principal and our efforts, making the change into an automatic process was not agreeable to some of them. A portion of these teachers felt they were already doing this type of intervention on their own. Others felt that they should not undergo a new process unless there was research proving it was effective. Finally, there were teachers who simply did not want to change what they had already established as their procedures in grade level meetings over the last 20 years. The degree of resistance from several teachers was something for which we were not prepared. We found ourselves in a position where we would receive a verbal barrage of dissatisfaction. The words of dissent, that would not reach the principal's ears directly, were leveled full throttle at us.

By Shelly's assessment, the fact that teachers now make grade level meetings an avenue of student discussion using Schools Attuned strategies constitutes evidence that schoolwide implementation of the Schools Attuned program has begun; however, it is understood that the program is still a work in progress.

To make sure that this work continues at our school, we will retain our roles as facilitators at the grade level meetings, focusing on students and Schools Attuned strategies. Each of us will see to it that the next step is reached pertaining to the follow up of students initiated with Schools Attuned strategies. We will continue to be advocates of the program, keeping it in the topics of conversations around the campus. Each of us can continue to promote the program by using the Schools Attuned format as classroom exercises and lessons with our students. By encouraging the terminology from Schools Attuned with students and staff, we expect to see it move forward in regular conversation.

Reflective Questions

- What roles are teacher leaders playing in your workplace?
- How do other teachers respond to teacher leaders in your workplace?
- In what ways can leadership teams engender more schoolwide ownership for initiatives designed to improve teaching and learning?

Teachers Educating Each Other

A leadership dense organization is characterized by quality mentoring and peer coaching and by adults challenging peers and themselves to think deeply about teaching and learning. The writings by two teacher leaders in this section clearly demonstrate this. Both Bonnie Jacobsen and Mary Beth Boyle have found places to be strong leaders in their communities.

Bonnie writes:

The summer held a sunny experience. I taught Complex Instruction[2] with a fellow coach to district teachers. It was the first time that either of us had done this without the "heavyweights" from Stanford assisting us. The district was supporting us and teachers were loving it. Complex Instruction is me! It promotes all the teaching that I think is best for students, especially in culturally, linguistically, and academically diverse classrooms.

We had taken all the components of the weeklong training in Complex Instruction and rearranged them in a way we thought was logical from a participant's point of view. We divided each day into theory sections and hands-on practice sections. Then we had to decide who would lead each section. We were scared to do the theory parts since that had always been done by the "experts." When we were teaching, we helped each other, and it went smoothly. The participants gave us great evaluations, and they are actually implementing it the next year.

Mary Beth writes:

A team of five elementary and secondary literacy coaches sat at a table, heads closely drawn together, intently discussing a student's essay.

"His interpretations are so right on!" one exclaimed.

"Yes, but the criteria we developed for what it means to meet the standard in this area also states that students must reference specific textual details to support their interpretations. Other than this one line, I don't see any support. Do you?"

This is a snippet of conversation I overheard at a recent professional development training my partner and I planned and facilitated for the literacy coaches in our district. They were engaged in learning a protocol for analyzing student work and the energy in the room was electric as educators closely and thoughtfully examined sixth graders' writing for clues to determine what students had learned about character analysis and what further instruction they needed to deepen their understanding.

This is meaningful professional development that will be even more meaningful when these literacy coaches take the process back to their sites and guide teachers through examinations of their own students' work, so different from the professional development that

I remember from my early career, which was either a smorgasbord of unrelated choices or a one-size-fits-all, full-day workshop. And this process is just one tool that our coaches learn to support them in doing their jobs well.

Ongoing professional development is not always in place, even in districts that have released exemplary teachers to work as coaches full-time. And it wasn't initially in place in ours either. In the model's first year, the literacy coaches received training in how to deliver the specific English language development (ELD)/literacy professional development program that the district had purchased. In addition, they received some excellent professional development to enhance their content knowledge in reading and literacy. What was missing, however, was sustained attention to how to build the skills that good coaches need to do their jobs well. And there was no plan in place for how to provide coaches with ongoing professional development throughout their tenure in the position.

As a former new teacher advisor, I appreciate the complexity of the coaching role and was so grateful for the model of ongoing support that the project had provided my colleagues and me as we made the shift from supporting students to supporting our colleagues. With this in mind, my partners and I created a plan for a monthly coaching institute that all of the literacy coaches would attend. We presented our plan to the district administrators in educational services and advocated for the needs of teacher leaders to continue to grow and build their expertise. Our plan was approved.

In each session, we try to balance time for coaches to problem-solve with each other about job-related issues they are encountering at their sites; time for professional reading or discussion or sharing best practices for reading and writing instruction to continue to build our content knowledge; and time for learning tools, language, and processes to support the daily work of one-on-one and small-group coaching and facilitation. So far this year we have shared strategies for how to enter and build a coaching relationship with a colleague, language that supports this relationship and that encourages the teacher to reflect more deeply on his/her own practice, a protocol for examining student work collaboratively with an eye toward what steps to take next instructionally, and some specific tools for collecting classroom observation data that is objective and focused.

One of the ways that I know this approach is having an impact is in the way that the coaches left the session I described in the opening vignette. Coaches left with specific plans and ideas for implementation at their sites. Three elementary coaches from the same site stayed after the meeting to discuss a plan for how they would share this information with their principals. Two middle school coaches saw a way to embed the process into the school-wide scoring of the district writing assessment that they would be facilitating the following week. Other coaches had plans for introducing the process to the grade level and department teams they work with at their sites.

Through the coaching institute, we have helped to create a space for true collegiality among the literacy coaches, and it is one of the things of which I am most proud in my work as a teacher leader.

Reflective Questions

- In what ways do you currently mentor others at your workplace? In what ways do others mentor you?
- How do you encourage others to think more deeply about their practice? Who encourages you to think more deeply and how does this person do it?
- Are there systems that you can put in place to nurture this goal?

Teachers as Advocates

In a leadership dense organization, teachers do not blame; instead they advocate for students, teachers, and parents. Margaret Butcher served as a new teacher advisor at her school district. What she writes below demonstrates the incredible growth she experienced as a teacher leader. (See Chapter 6 for more on advocacy.)

When I tell people that I'm a new teacher advisor, many are instantly envious. The position is well respected in our area. This respect gives me a strong position from which to advocate for new teachers. I also derive a sense that my work is valued and expected to be of high quality because my position is esteemed, well connected, and meaningful. As an advisor, I work with new teachers at most of the elementary schools in my district. Because I work at so many schools, I am able to have a broad view of policies and actual practice. I can draw on this grander view and translate it into context for new teachers, providing examples and comparisons from all over.

The key to the strength of the New Teacher Center is the high level of support provided to advisors, which we then may draw on to support our new teachers. Our weekly advisor meetings are a crucial feature of how we are supported, enabling us support others. These meetings are the heart of our own professional development, both paralleling and serving as a model for the professional development we do with the new teachers. The presentations and discussions at our meetings are designed and differentiated to be appropriate for our level(s) of experience in coaching adults. We discuss how to focus that coaching on the New Teacher Formative Assessment System and how to present trainings that simultaneously meet the needs of the teachers, the district, and the Beginning Teacher Support and Assessment (BTSA) standards. At these meetings, we also explore how and when to advocate for new teachers and when to encourage them to advocate for themselves. Each meeting exemplifies what a learning community looks and sounds like.

In the first years of teaching, unsatisfactory situations that require advocacy can take many forms: When the working conditions of the teachers are not equitable, the teachers feel undervalued, and the students are not able to learn in the environments they deserve. We have been instrumental in finding materials and furniture, seeing that the physical environment in the room is improved as necessary, and shepherding requests through channels that are familiar to an experienced teacher but not to a new teacher. In the spring, we set up a small-group meeting with the district superintendent and assistant superintendents to give new teachers a chance to say what has helped them in their development as a teacher during the year and what further support the district could provide. Change that came from these communications included a list of what should be part of every classroom when a new teacher moves in and, when there used to be a bit more money, a classroom set-up fund.

When the children who make up new teachers' classes are not familiar to them, teachers have to figure out how to differentiate and how to do it within a curriculum that they have not yet taught. We have a fundamental tool called the Analysis of Student Work. Through looking at student work with a rubric, we can determine together what the student strengths are and what particular skills should next be taught to each level. This process is now being incorporated as job-embedded professional development in grade level data teams across the district. Teachers have the opportunity to collaborate on choosing best practices and strategies and then to try them out together and support each other in promoting student achievement. Another issue about new teachers' assignments is that they are often hired close to or after the start of school. I have advocated in principals' meetings and with other administrators for new elementary teachers having the opportunity to concentrate on one grade in one room. I have also counseled against afterschool tutoring or coaching that gets in the way of lesson planning and site collaboration.

When the teacher's grade level or department does not meet regularly to collaborate, the teacher cannot benefit from peers' experience and may feel disaffected. In these situations, I have encouraged or facilitated further collaboration with the other grade level teachers, the resource specialist, the principal, or a student's parents. Encouraging these types of collaboration is my major contribution to new teachers finding their place in the learning community. At other times, I have attended the teachers' grade level meetings with them, just so they can have another set of ears and eyes there to help them make sense of the process.

When the principal is overworked (as they all are), the teacher may not have a clear picture of what is required of him or her. In this situation, I have encouraged a teacher to return to the goals he or she wrote, or the district's walk-through checklist, or the preparation sheet for a principal's observation, and be specific about what the principal should observe for or explain. Most often, the teacher wants to know what a certain requirement would look like in the classroom, and we work together on planning for that requirement. When we meet, I ask the principal to tell me what she or he is concerned about so that the teacher and I can work on clarification together. Sometimes, I request that the teacher be given release time to observe another teacher, me, or the principal demonstrating a lesson that incorporates the teaching standards that the principal is seeking.

Because I can see the efficacy of my work, I can keep on trying to do it better. It comes down to how well I can advocate for new teachers and their students in our district. I know it's working when I hear from teachers I've worked with, after their first few years, that they are confident and effective and making their own mentoring and leadership choices. I know my district is retaining more of its newly hired teachers than it did previously. I am honored to be part of an exceptional group of teacher leaders who make the district stronger by providing excellent professional development in its most effective, job-embedded form.

Reflective Questions

- How do teachers advocate for new teachers at your workplace?
- What evidence do you have for the impact of this advocacy?

Leading and Managing Change

Anyone who has gone crabbing knows that it is unnecessary to cap a crab bucket because as soon as one crab tries to scuttle out, the others drag it back down. Some faculties function the same way, actively resisting the efforts of any member to press beyond normal practice. (Duke, 1994, pp. 269–270)

Being a leader in a school that builds leadership capacity requires skills in working with the resistance and resisters. Often some teachers are resentful when other teachers step forward into leadership roles, and they need help accepting leadership from peers and accepting the personal responsibility to step forward themselves. The following story is especially powerful since these five teachers thought through their actions so carefully and the impact was so powerful. This narrative is long, but their leadership has had a huge impact on school practice and on student learning. Evelia Rosso, Margarida Oliveira, Joy Dvorak, Kristin Strand, and Christel Morley write:

In 2002, our school was in the midst of a comprehensive restructuring plan of our reading program. The staff was in the neutral zone

(Bridges, 1991), caught between the old program and the new. This transitional phase led to anxiety and resentment among teachers. Those who favored the old program became very protective of it, causing the staff to become immobilized. "Given the ambiguities of the neutral zone, it is natural for people to become polarized between those who want to rush forward and those who want to go back to the old ways" (Bridges, 1991, p. 35). Our master's group of five was also caught up in this tumultuous situation, wanting to move forward with the new reading program, yet finding resisters at every turn. We decided as a team to take a courageous step and help guide our school through the changes. We were taking a daring risk, for an immense challenge lay before us. If we planned carefully and strategically, we might successfully lead our school through the change, but the possibility of failure was very real to us. Would we be able to provide teachers with a process to improve student achievement in reading and at the same time guide them through this time of disruptive change? This question became the significant issue around systemic reform that we feel changed the direction of our school. Although initially focusing solely on teachers, we eventually included in the process additional stakeholders, such as parent volunteers and the English Language Acquisition Committee (ELAC).

First we wanted to initiate a feeling of collegiality among the teachers who were struggling to find common ground. We attempted to create an activity of common interest through a beautification project involving our multipurpose room. For years, this room had been a catch-all for old furniture, obsolete supplies, and custodians' tools. The walls had been neglected, displaying torn posters, tattered notes, and the attempted decor of years gone by. This central room was badly in need of overhaul in order to become a schoolwide showcase. The team cleaned up the room, stripping the walls of clutter and cleaning out storage rooms. In the process, we discovered hundreds of outdated textbooks; science, physical education, and art materials; and old but usable furniture. In this year of fiscal frugality, it was clear to us that these outdated materials could be recycled. To the delight of the staff, we organized a huge giveaway of materials. This activity was followed by a giveaway to parents. Teachers now exhibit the students' best work, transforming the room into an attractive academic showcase in which everyone takes pride. It was rewarding for the team to see the buy-in from teachers.

As a team, we met often, discussing and clarifying our vision for improving the morale at our school while at the same time improving student achievement. We formed a plan we felt might be successful. This plan would give individual teachers input; it would require very specific instructional strategies using assessment data; and it would offer support to all teachers who were agreeable to venture forth. Although we were anxious to offer the staff our process for improving reading achievement, we knew that we had to be patient and allow staff voices to be carefully listened to so that the feelings behind the words could be heard. Joy, Kristin, and Christel belonged to the School Leadership Team, an important vehicle for effecting school change.

We helped organize four focus groups during the initial staff development day of the 2003 school year. The purpose of these focus groups was to get problems or issues out in the open and to allow staff voices to be heard. The data from the discussions of the focus groups was recorded on chart paper and was later formatted for ease of use. We recognized that establishing a direction which would allow for total staff voice was a first positive step toward bridging the earlier turbulent times.

A subsequent staff development day was held in November. Our team agreed that not only would this day be a prime opportunity for us to provide teachers with a process to improve student achievement in reading, but it would potentially also be a pivotal day for us as leaders to guide our staff out of the neutral zone. A major concern for us was the uncertainty about whether we would be able to gain the support of teachers, especially that of the resisters who were still struggling with their insecurities in managing change. Our courage sprang from a feeling of commitment to our team vision and to each other *and* from an organizational strength that we all possessed. The plan was to be well prepared for this staff development day, making it as productive as possible. With that in mind, we volunteered through the vehicle of the School Leadership Team to organize and conduct the staff development day. Fortunately, our principal supported our initiative, entrusting us with the planning process, the implementation of the staff development day, and the subsequent debriefing.

First, we organized the data from the focus groups to create a survey that would address staff needs in a more detailed way. Using "People Connections" from Speck and Knipe (2005), the survey was designed to identify teachers who had ideas to share with staff members as well as those who needed further learning opportunities. Staff members were instructed to choose two items for a learning experience and two items to share with other staff members. The sessions were designed to incorporate these learners and sharers across grade levels in order to ensure that faculty members would make connections with other teachers they didn't normally talk with as a way of developing professional relationships.

The analysis of the survey then led to the design of sessions to be attended by teachers at the staff development day to be held in November. Recognizing the importance of individual choice, we narrowed the sessions to six options within four time slots. A large poster was created and made public to the staff as a sign-up for the stated sessions. After the sign-up sheet was completed, the information was presented in a user-friendly format to the staff, along with the day's agenda, two days prior to the November date.

The day began with a personal journal prompt to be completed by the entire staff about their expectations of the day ahead. The staff then attended four one-hour sessions facilitated by fellow teachers and staff members. In the role of school leaders, we strategically placed ourselves in the position of leading several of the sessions.

Margarida facilitated two sessions called "Centers and Management." During these sessions, she addressed the needs that staff members had for providing their students with differentiated, independent work during small group reading instruction. Not only did Margarida apply many of the strategies she employed in her own classroom, but she also gave each participant a comprehensive handout of activities.

Christel helped facilitate two sessions on peer coaching. This collaborative strategy was both a district focus and a key learning component for a core group of primary teachers to use to coach each other as we implemented new groupings for reading instruction.

Evelia, Kristin, Joy, and Christel presided over several workshops focusing on phonemic awareness and phonics. We were aware that all teachers had students in their classrooms that needed decoding help, but many teachers lacked the skills to teach phonics. In preparation for these workshops, our group collected an extensive file of lessons that would address phonemic awareness as well as phonics. These lessons were organized in a sequential order of difficulty. During each workshop, we first explained the process of teaching beginning phonics and then modeled many of the lessons and instructional strategies. The file of lessons was then made available for all staff members to use. The immediate benefit for teachers was the availability of ready-made lessons that had been aligned with our adopted assessment program. The phonics sessions during the staff development day were attended by almost all teachers and, to our delight, were well received. Even the resisters responded in a positive manner.

After all sessions were complete, the staff members were once again given a journal prompt to reflect upon the learnings that they would take with them into their classrooms. As a tool to continue the purposeful, ongoing staff development, a plus/delta chart was created to gather input on the day's events. The plusses included the following:

- Differentiated for teacher needs
- Choices were available
- Learners and sharers mixed together which encouraged learning from each other
- Time to share with each other
- Opportunity to meet with other grade levels
- Needs and expertise came from staff

Team reflection revealed that these plusses had been designed into the day. The objective of the day had been accomplished. As a positive conclusion to the day, facilitators and participants were thanked wholeheartedly and recognized for their efforts.

Our next steps were revealed through the staff's deltas. These included:

- A need to differentiate for levels of understanding
- Build in a make-and-take time
- More time for each session
- Reflection time at the end of each session
- Repeat sessions for missed opportunities
- Continue session format during staff meeting time in order to keep momentum going and have additional time to share with each other.

While the team felt much positive feedback came from the plusses, the deltas were equally exciting due to the matched staff and team vision for providing mutual support, collaboration, and staff voice.

An ongoing component in providing teachers with a process to improve student achievement in reading was our action research project (ARP). The problem revealed by our ARP was that more than half of first, second, and third grade students scored below grade level in reading. Beginning in the fall of 2003 and continuing into the winter of 2004, we fervently gathered reading test results from all students in the three grade levels. This data was formatted in Excel, which could easily sort test results by skill levels, and formed the basis of grouping students for reading instruction. The process required teachers to spend time in collaboration to consider the placement of each student. Flexible groupings were then established, and teachers used phonics and phonemic awareness skills to differentiate instruction. At the teachers' disposal were the phonics lessons we had gathered and presented at the previous staff development day. These lessons would address specific phonics skills as indicated by the assessment results. The primary teachers expressed their satisfaction with having the file of lessons as a means of driving their instruction. For us, this was an exciting moment since grouping students for very precise skills instruction using assessment data was essential to our vision of improving student achievement in reading.

In his book *Managing Transitions* (1991), William Bridges states that in order for people to function successfully in the neutral zone, we need to provide such things as seminars and team building. Our focus groups and staff development tactics supplied these components and assisted teachers in maneuvering through the neutral zone. We also felt that time management support would alleviate much of the stress teachers felt with the new reading program demands. Consequently, we recruited more than 20 parent volunteers and trained them in the process of assessing individual students in phonics and phonemic awareness. Although we felt strongly that teachers would greatly benefit from this parental support, our principal's behavior was more reserved. The effect of this training, however, was a pleasant surprise all around. The parents felt privileged to be approached and to share in the educational process at their children's school. The teachers were elated with the amount of time that they saved as a result of being assisted by these very capable parent helpers. To our satisfaction, our principal saw the advantage of having a strong cadre of parent volunteers at our disposal.

By providing the staff with an opportunity for collegiality, occasions to be heard through surveys, focus groups, and staff development, and by offering them skills, strategies, and materials to use for their reading instruction, as well as a way to address individual student needs, we feel we have helped guide them successfully through the neutral zone. We have learned that change happens slowly, as it is a process that must be molded and shaped to the needs of the stakeholders. There are still teachers at our school who embrace teaching "for the way things used to be." Many teachers, however, have moved forward with the new reading program. One only has to listen to their conversations in the staff room as they share their success stories to know that this is true. We have learned that leadership means taking risks. But in so doing and in persevering, change can and does happen. Finally, we have learned that action research is an awesome catalyst for influencing school improvement. At our school, at least three grade levels (about 18 teachers) have garnered the benefits of our action research project. As we analyze the last pieces of data and close the final pages of our ARP, we sincerely hope that this is not the end of one solitary project but the beginning of many more to come, as future school leaders join us in our endeavor to create the very best school for our children.

Reflective Questions

- How do teachers demonstrate resistance to change?
- How does your school deal with teacher resistance?

APPLYING THE CONCEPTS IN YOUR WORKPLACE

1. Continue to read and to share reflections on this reading with your colleagues.

2. Continue and broaden the teacher reflection group. Maintain norms and practices of trust so that participants can reflect on and share "how they are learning to lead."

3. Use the writings and reflective questions in this chapter to start the conversations. Again, we hope that a primary value of this book will be that groups of people will read it together and use the writing of these teachers to reflect and create opportunities to grow as leaders.

4. Volunteer for leadership roles and ask for mentoring and feedback.

5. If you are in a leadership role, recruit others to lead with you and serve as a mentor to them. Give them important roles to play and help them be successful.

6. Help to institute a leadership team at your workplace. Insist on and model quality meeting skills and facilitation skills. If your school has a functioning leadership team, help organize an evaluation process that assesses the impact of this team on student and teacher learning. Tools for the evaluation can be found in Lambert (2003a).

7. Create opportunities for teachers to share their expertise and help provide the resources, including time, so that this sharing becomes the core of job-embedded, professional development.

8. Help establish formal school norms that stress the importance of conversations being positive and constructive.

ESSENTIAL QUESTIONS

1. Think of a time when the principal tried to "be all things for all people." How was the depth of commitment to initiatives shallow and not sustained?

2. Think of a time when leadership was shared at your school and the leadership was skillful and purposeful. In what ways was the commitment to initiatives deeper?

3. How did it impact student learning?

RESOURCES

Tools

There are excellent tools for assessing teacher leadership in Katzenmeyer and Moller's books (1996, 2001) and in Lambert's book (2003a).

The Speck and Knipe book (2005) is an outstanding source on professional development practices.

Complex Instruction: cgi.stanford.edu/group/pci/cgi-bin/site.cgi

Organizations

Schools Attuned: www.schoolsattuned.org

New Teacher Center: The New Teacher Center (NTC) at the University of California Santa Cruz is a national resource dedicated to teacher induction, development, new teacher training, and the support of programs and practices that promote excellence and diversity in America's teaching force. www.newteachercenter.org

SURVEY

The following survey was developed by Donna Emerson, Bindi Gill, and Judith Hutchison, teachers at Marshall Lane School in Campbell Union School District. They wanted feedback about how their peers perceived they had grown as leaders. They learned that the staff thought their ARP was important and that most teachers thought that the three of them had grown as leaders. However, they learned from this survey that some teachers felt uninformed about the project. They felt by doing the survey, they modeled the importance of asking for feedback.

HOW DID WE DO? — A TEACHER SURVEY

Our Triple L team wants to know if we grew as much as we thought. Did we annoy you? Did we excite you? Did we do anything of importance? We would like to know. Please, please, take a moment of your precious time (believe us; we know it's precious) to complete this user-friendly survey.

Thank you, Gracias, Grazie, Merci beaucoup, Danke Schon

How Did We Do? — A Teacher Survey[*]

On a scale of 1–5, where *1* is *Not at all* and *5* is *A great deal*, please give us your opinion by circling the corresponding number.

1. Did you notice that we, as individuals, showed professional growth (took on more tasks, spoke up more at meetings, took risks)?

   1   2   3   4   5

2. Did you notice that we, as individuals, exhibited personal growth (personality, collegiality, resiliency)?

   1   2   3   4   5

3. Did you notice that we, as a team, exhibited professional growth?

   1   2   3   4   5

4. Did you know what our research project was about?

   1   2   3   4   5

5. Do you think analyzing the effectiveness of our Jumpstart Program was important?

   1   2   3   4   5

[*] When you turn it in, don't forget to pick up some goodies!

(Name optional) _____

ENDNOTES

1. Schools Attuned is a comprehensive professional development and service program that offers educators new methods for recognizing, understanding, and managing students with differences in learning.

2. Complex Instruction evolved from over 20 years of research by Elizabeth Cohen, Rachel Lotan, and their colleagues at the Stanford School of Education. The goal of this cooperative learning strategy is to provide academic access and success for *all* students in heterogeneous classrooms.

CHAPTER THREE

Influencing Student Learning

Enduring Understandings

- Skillful teacher leaders collaboratively plan instruction, aiming at continuous improvement of students' learning.
- Schools are most effective in meeting students' learning needs when leaders focus on and skillfully mobilize institutional and community resources for such a purpose.

It is not enough to have a good mind; the main thing is to apply it well.

(Descartes, 1998, p. 1)

C losing the Academic Achievement Gap (CTAG) became the dictum of school reformers in the last decades of the twentieth century and continues to shape today's reform efforts. Indeed, for many educators, closing the achievement gap has turned out to be the central goal by which to gauge equity outcomes in schools. By the end of the 1990s, CTAG was mobilizing the grass roots reform movement—both as a rallying cry and as a desired goal—and in many cases had become a stated goal of official state and federal top-down initiatives, as well as an explicit goal of many schools and school districts. The No Child Left Behind Act uses this noble goal to justify its draconian accountability provisions. Teacher leaders find themselves at the center of the CTAG efforts.

Research has consistently shown that closing the achievement gap is related to a wide variety of intrinsic and extrinsic factors. Research focused on *extrinsic* factors has looked at the influence of socioeconomic family status, parents' educational level, emotional and physical care of newborn children, and cultural contexts. Research focused on *intrinsic* factors has primarily shown the relation between closing the achievement gap and classroom practices, school culture, teachers' belief and value systems, and racial and cultural dynamics in the school. This chapter centers on the intrinsic factors, for we believe academic success has to do more with what exists within a school than with what is outside and that while important, the latter supports the former.

While not entirely conclusive, some researchers and experts (e.g., Darling-Hammond, 1997; Hertert, 2003) have argued that the single most important factor in closing the achievement gap appears to be teachers' professional preparation, including credentialing programs they attended, professional development, subject matter knowledge, and teaching expertise. As the narratives below show, well-educated and prepared teachers who believe in their students' capacity to learn and succeed act as agents in supporting each other, helping students control their own learning, and bringing coherence between students' needs and the use of the school's resources.

CLOSING THE ACHIEVEMENT GAP
AND HABITS OF MIND

Our theory of action is that skillful teaching and leadership translate into increased learning for all students. This assertion puts the locus of control squarely on what happens in the classroom and when leadership capacity is fostered school-wide, to what happens in the school as a whole. We view this as a professional commitment to teaching and learning that engages students' high-order thinking, which leads to higher academic performance.

Teaching students to use their minds and hearts well refers to schooling aimed at creating intellectual habits and high moral and ethical conduct that will remain with them for the rest of their lives. Sizer (1992), Meier (1995), and Costa and Kallick (2000) describe habits of mind as acting intelligently toward new and unsuspected challenges. The authors identify a series of habits that can be summarized in Meier's (1995, p. 55) five habits:

1. How do we know what we know? (Evidence).

2. Who's speaking? (Perspective).

3. What causes what? (Cause and effect).

4. How might things have been different? (Hypothesis).

5. Who cares? (Empathy).

Habits of mind and habits of heart cement the knowledge articulated through the teaching of subject matter. They criss-cross every single subject, as well as the social life governing schools. We believe that schooling has little or no meaning if the ways in which we teach and learn have no relation to the intellectual discipline (habits of mind) and the behavior we exhibit (habits of heart). As the five habits listed above imply, teaching and learning deal with our day-to-day testing of

53

ideas (as in conducting research); building the necessary evidence (as in products created through assignments) to show what and how we know things; looking at an issue from multiple sides (as in explaining the "other"); being able to sympathize with other people's celebrations, wonders, and suffering (as in the study of the civil rights movement); and being able to connect the dots of a particular phenomenon (as in identifying the why of things).

In sum, teaching these habits ultimately results in narrowing the achievement gap. This means that academic performance will increase for all students by making sure that those in the bottom steadily rise to the performance level of the high achievers. Four components make up this theory of action:

1. Teachers believe that students can release their full intellectual potential. A nonnegotiable principle for teachers, and especially those in leadership positions, is to truly believe and demonstrate that all children can and do learn. Impacting student learning begins with the will of teachers to both imagine students' potential and find ways to provide them with the mechanisms appropriate to fulfill such potential.

Melissa Sherman, a high school English teacher, reflects on this issue the following way:

My goal as an educator is not only to teach my students to appreciate literature but for them to leave my classroom with a fuller heart, so that they too can pour out upon others. Not all students receive a fuller heart in the same way. For some, just communicating fills their heart. For others, what fills their heart may be the better understanding they receive about the world around them or the confidence gained in a job well done.

As an educator, I want to help students build dreams and see what they themselves cannot see. One of my favorite quotes is by Antoine de Saint-Exupery[1] "A rock pile ceases to be a rock pile, the moment a single man contemplates it bearing within him the image of a cathedral." I see each of my students as cathedrals. There is so much more to them than they see for themselves. I want my students to see themselves for what they are and to envisage dreams from that moment on.

54

Melissa's seamless teaching of appreciation of literature and the "filling" of students' hearts so that "they too can pour out upon others," highlights one key fact: As a teacher leader, she has the *determination* to show youngsters how to grow, simultaneously, rational and emotional habits. For her, the metaphorical "heart" connotes values such as compassion and love to humankind. While demanding academic rigor, she does not fall into the traditional binary entities, "mind" and "heart" (i.e., reason and emotion); instead, she sees both as unified parts of the human experience.

Being able to help a student envision beyond the individual's present into her or his future potential—from rock pile to cathedral—and building such future from where she or he stands—is at the core of good teaching. Ms. Sherman appears determined to create a powerful classroom experience for all—students and herself.

As Melissa's reflection suggests, teacher leaders confront internal and external forces that get in the way of powerful learning, but they unequivocally deal with these challenges. In the last analysis, Ms. Sherman led her actions from her own convictions and from what she understood were the challenges and promises. In other words, beliefs constitute the teacher leader's prime onus; everything else necessarily is subordinated to those beliefs.

Reflective Questions

- What role does imagination play in Melissa's reflective essay?
- How would you describe Melissa's belief?
- Which cathedrals are you building?

---

2. Teachers explicitly teach habits of mind and heart. Teaching this way requires teachers to be constantly alert to students' learning modalities and to understand that students must have a great deal of control over their own learning. In order to effectively increase learning, good teachers have the ability to identify students' specific academic and social challenges and needs.

Sally B. Peck, at the time of this writing a fifth grade teacher leader, offers her experience as a classroom leader who sought how to instill precisely the control of one's learning as a habit. She sought the connection between specific students' needs and challenges and the new knowledge and skills that leaders like her draw from a variety of sources (e.g., brain research, social science, and developmental psychology). This is what she wrote:

Empowering students by helping them understand their learning process is an important component of a differentiated classroom. Typically, each year elementary school students change teachers, while middle and high school students may change instructors each period. Thus, understanding how one learns best is essential in maturing as a student and as a teacher. Learning to take charge of how one learns and being able to communicate this in a classroom can empower students to consider their own learning styles and find success in school.

Recognizing the need to "chunk"[2] information from a textbook or a class lecture before studying for a test or to "subvocalize"[3] a chapter in history are simple but powerful strategies to help students take control of their individual learning strengths and understand their challenges. Applying learning strategies in the classroom or using accommodations to make learning more manageable and a less stressful experience is important for young students to understand. Educating youngsters about how and why people learn differently not only provides a mutual understanding but creates a more empathetic classroom atmosphere.

After two years of graduate research on writing in the elementary school classroom, I introduced a program for improving students' writing process and mechanics through the implementation of Writers' Workshop. In addition, I used portfolios to document student work and assess on an ongoing basis. Although many of these students had attended the same elementary school since first grade, their writing abilities were varied. Indeed, standardized test scores at my school reflected a dip in this area. I identified this writing program as one which could effectively be used with the entire class and allow for individual entry points and individual growth where it was needed. I wasn't disappointed in my choice for my class. After sharing my results with my colleagues, fourth grade teachers implemented it the following year.

Simultaneously, I had been consistently using the materials found in Dr. Mel Levine's Schools Attuned[4] program with my fifth grade students. Daily conversation using the vocabulary and terminology found in this program were common practices in my classroom. I found stories about student experiences in Levine's *Keeping Ahead in School* (1990). These stories launched deep and worthwhile classroom conversations about differences in learning. In addition, I identified a few students in the classroom who would benefit from one-on-one time to discuss aspects of their learning and help guide them to better understand their individual strengths and weaknesses. Together, we would then identify strategies to use in their studies to accommodate their learning growth. Many of these strategies were not only about helping one student succeed but about good teaching practices. Many of these techniques ultimately benefited other students in the same class.

Michael was a child who avoided writing whenever possible, and his "graphomotor"[5] skills were weak. He was left-handed and a "C" student in writing. In isolation, his writing mechanics were strong, but he was inconsistent in applying the skills to his writing efforts. It was obvious to me as his teacher that Michael was exceptionally bright. His interpretations and discussions about stories we'd read during guided reading were outstanding and his imagination in oral conversation top notch. In November, Michael and I spoke about his mature comprehension and his creativity in conversation. We agreed that this strength as a student was not evident when he wrote his ideas on paper. As an accommodation, and with the support of his parents, we agreed to allow Michael the use of a computer keyboard as a tool to facilitate his writing. Although his keyboarding skills were not perfect, we saw this opportunity as a long-term goal for the year to help Michael better communicate his mature ideas and thoughts. It did not take long to observe noticeable improvement in his efforts, both in the classroom and at home. He became a more willing writer; and when he began receiving positive feedback from home and school, his desire to put greater effort into his written work snowballed. The mechanics of writing also improved because he was finding the writing process less tedious and painful. His end-of-the-year portfolio contained some of the best written work in our fifth grade class. Simply intervening and allowing Michael the use of a keyboard to reflect his "voice" was a powerful example of how honoring an individual learning style and managing the available tools and environment can help a student find success in the classroom.

Another student who found success was Max. Max was a fifth grade student who seemed to have his hand in the air continually and always had something to say in class conversations. He had a reputation for being too talkative with his peers in the classroom and in discussions within the classroom. On the outside, it would appear that Max wanted to dominate conversations and did not understand the amount of time he was taking from others who also might want to share. Despite the mature comments and clear artic-ulations Max offered orally, his written assessments didn't reflect a student with strong and mature understandings. He was a child who demonstrated independence in his studying and rarely requested assistance in his work; homework efforts in studying for tests or quizzes were very poor. In conversations, Max shared with me that he did not want help in his studying and was quite happy to study alone at his desk in his bedroom. This was a child who clearly demonstrated strength in his verbal skills. He was a student who needed to leverage his strengths to support his weaker memory issues in his learning. As a class, we had discussed the importance in understanding that people learn differently and often need dif-ferent tools and methods to facilitate their growth as students. Max and I agreed that one of his strengths lay in his verbal skills, and we agreed that he would use this strength in studying for his tests and quizzes, whether it be at school or at home. It also became appar-ent that Max's consistent need to verbalize was his way of process-ing to help with memory. In a group conference with his parents, Max agreed to use support from his parents, older sister, or peers to help him when he had to study for tests or quizzes. The following quarter, Max's grades in social studies rose considerably. Needless to say, Max was very proud of himself and his efforts to use his learning strengths to feel more successful in school. He was the first to share with his classmates during our class conversations on learning styles about how he'd found a way to be more effective in his studying.

Students arrive at school each day with a wide range of learning strengths and weaknesses. Each classroom is full of students with a diverse range of needs requiring educational care, and it is possible to recognize and meet these individual needs in the classroom without segregation or stigmatization. For many students, it is the teacher who needs to help navigate the way to identify the roads for the child to feel success. Students may not have the words, the clear understanding, and/or the confidence to discuss an area of school that is challenging them, yet they are often all too familiar with the anxiety and stress connected to their struggle. I have seen how educating my students through simple conversations has empowered them with the knowledge they deserve and need to become better advocates for themselves as students. Combined with various individual accommodations, I believe a classroom can be a place of success for the great majority of children.

Reflective Questions

- What does "empowering students" mean in Ms. Peck's story?
- How can you raise questions about differentiating instruction at your site?
- How can you translate from Ms. Peck's experience to your own in helping students to identify their learning modes by themselves?

3. Teachers foster a climate of collective planning so that they learn good practices from each other, address the less successful ones, and plan large units for understanding. The existence of this cooperation must be intentional, in terms of allocating the time and resources to nurture it and in terms of facilitating processes that allow teachers to incorporate collaboration into their day-to-day preoccupations.

Susan Bedford is a teacher leader who mentors new and veteran colleagues in her high school district. Due to a consistent allocation of time and human talent, her school district employs leaders such as Susan to provide meaningful support at the classroom level throughout the school year. Mature teachers like her coach new and not-so-new, challenged teachers throughout the school year in a program called Beginning Teacher Support and Assistance (BTSA).

Curriculum discussions, the lifeblood of any good school, can take place on a school level or a district level. At my high school, discussions of curriculum took place in a variety of ways and locations. There were, of course, casual discussions and lesson plan and test trading, as in "Do you have anything on *Romeo and Juliet*?" These questions, while they represent collaboration on a very basic, sketchy level, don't get at important ideas about curriculum. They are "survival" discussions, often in the lunchroom or hallway, in which one overworked teacher helps another or one experienced teacher mentors a new faculty member.

The second level of curriculum discussion takes place at a deeper, more formal level. Often these discussions were between a history teacher and an English teacher or perhaps small groups of grade-alike teachers in those departments. Out of these collaborative discussions grew many excellent joint projects such as a Senior Exhibition, a junior year American Dream project, and so on. These discussions tended to ask what kids need to know and be able to do and often focused on an end-of-unit or end-of-year assessment, usually a big project.

A third kind of curricular collaboration involved pairs or teams of teachers planning for jointly structured classes, such as the humanities class I taught. A colleague and I developed a joint English/Modern World History program for freshmen honors students, which later was used as a model for similar courses for college prep students and at other schools. I spent many hours in meetings with my colleague planning detailed curriculum, and those were among the most rewarding hours of my career.

We, as the BTSA coaches, provide new teachers with a wealth of information about instructional strategies. We hold two days of training for new teachers before school opens. We provide information about planning, about establishing classroom procedures, and about management (discipline) techniques, and we model many strategies teachers can use in their classrooms. We meet with teachers weekly and observe their classes frequently. Many of our conversations center around instructional strategies and reflecting on what techniques worked and what can be improved next time. We have afterschool meetings, held four times a year, which often focus on or model instructional strategies that new teachers can adapt to their classrooms. New teachers join their colleagues in discussing the three domains of teaching—curriculum, assessment, and instruction—at grade and department levels.

Reflective Questions

- How different is spontaneous collaboration and organized collaboration for leading classroom work?
- What kind of practice predominates at your site?
- How can you move your practice to the third type described by Ms. Bedford?

---

4. Teachers define priorities differently. This assertion implies two things: (a) valuing the staff and (b) focusing material and human resources on increasing the learning of all students. Making these two points the center of a school's action plan conveys an unambiguous commitment to creating an environment where just and equitable outcomes matter. It also means that the allocation of such resources will follow a clear commitment to the continuous renewal of the learning experience for every single child and adult. Learning for all marks, in this sense, the direction of everyday actions.

VALUING THE STAFF

Teacher leadership is deeply linked to the existence of positive learning environments, where every member of the school's community accounts for his or her work, where the issue of students' work and performance dominates the daily conversations, and topics such as racial, gender, and social class privilege are all part of ordinary discourse. Embedding teacher learning into daily practice, validating and making explicit the knowledge teachers produce, and approaching such learning as the work of a whole school are all premises at the core of a new approach to professional development.

Donna Peltz, Gordon Jack, Madeline Miraglia, Steve Kahl, and Tim Farrell, a team of high school teachers, write about how they addressed narrowing the achievement gap and, in the process, they examine the growth of their team's leadership.

Our high school is one of two comprehensive high schools in our city's high school district. The district serves a community population of 67,000. The attendance area includes large, predominantly residential portions of three cities. The school has a current enrollment of 1,636. Of these students, about 6 out of every 10 identify themselves as Caucasian, and the rest as either Asian or Latino.

When we first gathered as members of an Urban High School Leadership (UHSL) Team, we already had so much in common, both personally and professionally. Each of us shared a passion for teaching students to be competent and conscientious young adults, yet we each had taken different approaches. Donna had just recently been selected as a vice principal in charge of professional development, among other things. Tim had been teaching history for five years and was inspiring students on social justice matters. Madeline brought a wealth of expertise as coach from her participation in the Facing History and Ourselves Program. Gordon, an English teacher, coordinates the district's efforts for new teachers to master the state's standards. And Steve is a noted professional development facilitator on differentiated curriculum in our region.

As we began to outline our action plan, we realized that we first had to understand how to work together, to communicate, and to bring our differences to bear. As we learned to work effectively, we created a shared vision of the school's direction. We examined the idea of measuring and bringing about a "cultural shift" at our school. We decided that professional development would be the vehicle through which such a shift could occur. Thus we committed to the evaluation of professional development as a strategy to improve teaching and learning at our school. We figured this could be the way to "see" a cultural shift and its effects on student learning. We asked the question: How much more regularly might teachers use "best practices" with their students as a result of their involvement in professional development at the school?

Last summer, our principal called on our team to help in the design of professional development for the year around the goal of narrowing the achievement gap. We became the school professional development committee. To address the needs of teachers seeking meaningful staff development, the committee on professional development altered the structure of inservice days to provide teachers with some choices. As a result, groups formed around such topics as "Brain Research," "Fred Jones' Tools for Teaching," "Differentiation," and "Project-Based Learning." Within each group, the facilitators used resource materials from the Association for Supervision and Curriculum Development (ASCD) to organize the time around purposeful and meaningful work. Moreover, the committee provided additional meeting procedures and organized a culminating gallery walk to educate fellow staff members on what was learned and accomplished. Although it was time efficient to plan among the six of us, we now realize that we left an entire group out of the process: the members of what had been the Professional Development Committee in previous years. Previously, the school improvement program coordinator and several teachers from the Science, Social Studies, and English Departments planned all professional development experiences for staff. We never officially disbanded that group; instead, we simply supplanted it.

Consequently, several department coordinators expressed discomfort at our new plan, wondering why these "new" people had suddenly taken over the reins of professional development and why the previous committee had no voice. Although our plan for the second year was sound, we had more trouble than should have been necessary convincing the coordinators of its worth. At first, some of us were a bit indignant about the resistance, but Kouzes and Posner (2002) reminded us, "People must believe that leaders understand their needs and have their interests at heart. Leadership is a dialogue, not a monologue" (p. 15).

Realizing this, we turned to texts such as William Bridges's (1991) *Managing Transitions* to create several approaches to help the administration manage the change dynamics that our new professional development entailed. As part of the same effort, we improved the effectiveness of the previous year by providing more rationale for the changes that were being made and more scaffolding to assist staff members in carrying out the new professional development methodology. For example, we decided to "treat the past with respect" by providing staff members with a retrospective of approaches to professional development over the last several years, identifying what was gained from each of the former initiatives.

Because we know that individual teachers also need support in transitions, our group developed and implemented several structures to support teachers in their differentiated learning. Each teacher, for example, used a template to design learning activities for each of the professional development days throughout the school year. In addition, we increased accountability by providing teachers with a second template in which they have been required to document their progress through each professional development experience this year.

Finally, we developed the professional development partner (PDP) approach, which pairs each adult learner with an adult learner from a different department. At the end of each professional development day, pairs got together to discuss their progress. To clarify the roles of the PDPs, we provided a list of model characteristics of a mutually supportive PDP meeting to the principal, who passed them on to the entire staff. We instituted this component because we believed in the value of shared learning with colleagues in a different department. A quote from Linda Lambert (2003a) captures our own feelings:

> It is important for educators to recognize the connection between our own learning and that of our colleagues. When we think in terms of reciprocity, we understand that we are responsible for our own and our colleagues' learning as well as that our students. This mutuality is at the heart of professional development. (p. 21)

Since we value the notion of building equity in our community, we decided to focus on the evaluation of professional development, as it seems to be the most powerful way to close the achievement gap at our school. Like most schools with ethnically diverse student populations, ours does not serve African American and Latino students as well as it serves White and Asian American.

Steve organized a subgroup of teachers, parents, community members, and administrators to meet and develop a problem-based learning (PBL) strategy to examine school issues. They identified key strategies that work best at narrowing the achievement gap, and the menu for professional development choices reflected the research findings exactly in the following year.

Once the PBL group finished its research, our team worked with other individuals to present the findings to the whole staff in May 2003. We carefully detailed the achievement gap, the PBL process up to that point, the research findings, and the implied agenda for professional development in the subsequent year. To end that staff meeting, we asked each staff member to examine the research findings to identify one way in which he or she could resolve to improve teaching practice in order to narrow the achievement gap. In doing so, we used research, reflection, and action in order to maximize learning for all students.

Conclusions

As we end our second year, we recognize the importance of carefully passing the torch to the next group of folks who will make decisions about our professional learning. We plan to end this school year by including a wide array of staff members in the planning for the following year, thereby expanding the recently tight circle of staff members who make the decisions. Through interviews, we have involved more stakeholders, as we have instituted a working protocol of a response mechanism that should outlast our team's work.

The format used this year for professional development has encouraged teachers to be self-reliant and to understand that passivity during professional development work limits success. The degree to which the staff participated in the professional development varies. Anecdotal information indicates that while some groups were very focused and continued meeting outside of designated professional development days, other teams used the time to socialize, lesson plan, or grade students' assignments.

Individuals chose to study a teaching methodology that they believed would help them in narrowing the achievement gap. Every staff member is in charge of his or her learning, reinforcing the notion that each of us is a competent professional capable of making choices about how to improve teaching practice.

Reflective Questions

- How did this team negotiate their relationships with its members, with the school's administration, with the faculty?
- How would you have negotiated your working relation with this team if you had been the person(s) who used to organize the school's professional development?
- What advantages and disadvantages do you see in this team's job-embedded professional development approach?

Focusing Resources

Distributing money, material resources, and people's talents and skills around classrooms does not automatically lead to closing the achievement gap. It is the equitable and purposeful distribution that yields results. We submit that it is the purposeful implementation of a school's mission and vision and the coherence between resources and carefully identified goals that form the most certain way for school resources to impact student learning.

Many school leaders know that their school's resources are inadequate and work to identify additional funding sources. Over time, a series of state, federal, and private foundation initiatives promoting the reform of schools have encouraged school leaders to aggressively seek such resources. The No Child Left Behind Act (NCLB) is one current example. NCLB has caused school districts to redirect massive amounts of resources to prepare students for tests mandated by the law. One of the results of this situation is that many schools are trying to implement too many programs and taking on multiple responsibilities without having a coherent strategy for using these resources. Few teachers and, sadly, few school leaders can articulate how various initiatives fit together coherently to impact student learning. The result is lack of school and district focus and, therefore, much bewilderment and anxiety on the part of teachers.

Teacher leaders facilitate conversations on coherence as a way to understand the seemingly disparate efforts within a school. They look at how resources are focused on the school's vision. They are able to travel between the big picture and the microlevel of programs, activities, and discrete interventions. Teacher leaders follow three steps to address coherence issues:

1. Identify the resources available to the school by asking:
   - What (program, activity, intervention) exists at the site? List institutions, organizations, and programs presently working at the site.
   - How is the school district involved?

2. Link the resources to the school's focus and vision by asking:
   - What kind of work have these activities, organizations, programs currently set in motion at the school?
   - What department, individuals, or programs are involved? (Who is responsible for what?)

3. Keep what is most likely to impact student learning and let go of unnecessary work by asking:
   - How are these programs, activities, and interventions helping the school achieve its focus and vision? And how are they not?
   - How can we let go of this (program, activity, intervention) without compromising our long-term relationships with the donating agency?

One useful tool teacher leaders have implemented to organize their findings from the above questions is the "coherence tool" (see Resources section at end of chapter), an aide that allows them to track and match needs to resources.

Successful teacher leaders engage the community in a constructivist and empowering fashion. *Constructivist* here means that communities are considered "sources of knowledge that educators need to access in order to understand the cultural, social, and linguistic barriers that separate schools from the communities they serve" (Arriaza, 2004, p. 14). *Empowering* means that schools and communities establish a relation of mutual respect, whereby the community is conceived as holding unbound transformative power and participates within its specific sphere of responsibility with children. Communities, in this view, work as coequal partners with the school's mission (Arriaza, 2004). In sum, teacher leaders understand and seek to tap into the wealth of knowledge, wisdom, and capacity embedded in a community's culture. At the end of the day, closing the achievement gap is about focusing all resources in order to teach students to use their minds well for, as Descartes said, having a mind is not enough.

Carlos O. Gómez, a teacher leader at a small charter high school, tells us what happened at his school when it was well supported by its parental and surrounding communities but resources were not clearly focused. While the story is a little long, the complexity of issues Mr. Gómez raise appear of great interest to us all. Enjoy!

Our school found itself in an unusual situation when opening its doors for the first time in 2001. Being the new child of a nonprofit, intermediary, services-oriented giant organization, the school instantly inherited a slew of special programs offered to its constituents and community. School leaders, severely under-staffed, believed that having access to so many community-based programs would hasten the social development and in turn the academic progress of its unique student population. Comprised primarily of Latino (Mexican and Mexican American) students living in one of the toughest areas of our huge city, the school was to be the model of the perfect marriage between strong commu-nity relationships tied to multiple services and the small school model.

Within the first three months of school, school leaders and staff found themselves in a state of disarray. The school's major problems rested in not being able to completely integrate the programs already housed within the nonprofit's Youth Center and our high school's operational site and trying to accommodate the many helping hands in the form of additional programs, private foundations, and community connections knocking at the front door. Teachers and students quickly lost enthusiasm and energy.

Similarly, teachers felt at odds with a schedule that included a 30-minute "Advisory" class, an almost hour long "Leadership" elec-tive class that had no set curriculum, and a one-hour mandatory "Tutorial" class after school for all students. At a structural level, the school was more like a large traditional comprehensive high school disguised as a small school.

We all participated in the design of a new schedule. By the end of its first year, the school had reorganized itself such that the task of building school structure and implementing a schoolwide discipline plan had taken priority over stacking the curriculum with energy-depleting courses. In spite of the school's mission statement that calls for leadership and personal excellence from students,[6] school leaders had to temporarily step to the side and truly consider the question, "What should be our focus right now?" The school's survival over the course of its first year came about more as the result of trial and error than anything else. School leaders like me applied a coherence tool (see Resources at end of chapter) to identify the programs in place that did not make sense to the school's focus. What follows are some of the discoveries we made while utilizing this tool.

Community and School Setting

As an agency, our nonprofit organization was established 40 years ago by a group of Chicano activists looking to curtail police brutality aimed at Mexican and Mexican American residents. Through the years, this organization grew as a nonprofit agency and is now responsible for providing accessible, culturally appropriate, and quality programs to youths, families, and seniors of our county.

Our small school is located in a clearly segregated area. It's physically separated from other communities on its southern, western, and eastern sides by three eight-lane highways. Over the last 30 years, the area's decline in home values has been steady. In addition, the community is known as a Norteño haven, a group of gangs formed of Mexican Americans.

Community and School Demographics

Using the 2000 Census, school leaders were able to obtain the funds they needed to forecast the number of students they could expect for each successive class, representing the ethnic compositions of the community. First, the city as a whole (924,950 residents) comprises the following:

- 3.3% African American
- 3.9% "Other"
- 26.6% Asian
- 30.2% Hispanic
- 36.0% White

In comparison, the same Census showed that our community comprises the following:

- 80% Hispanic
- 14% Asian/Pacific Islander
- 3% White
- 2% African American
- 1% "Other"

Beginning the fall of 2003 with its third batch of 50 freshmen, the school was ethnically represented in the following manner:

- Ninth grade class (50 students): 98% Hispanic/Latino, 2% White
- Tenth grade class (46 students): 90% Hispanic/Latino, 5% multiracial, 5% Asian/Pacific Islander
- Eleventh grade class (38 students): 92% Hispanic/ Latino, 8% multiracial.

To school officials, these numbers were clearly not representative of the community and especially the city as a whole. The student demographics by program showed the following for the 2002–2003 academic year:

- 56% English Language Learners (ELL)
- 85.7% of the student population qualified for free and reduced lunch (an increase of 42% from the previous year)

With the above numbers in mind, the staff then proceeded to create a map of all of the school and agency resources that could be used to better service this population.

Material, Economic, and Human Resources at the Site

Obtaining an organizational chart of the agency was the first item. School staff then retrieved information on the 10 other programs (not including our small charter high school) under the umbrella of the city's Youth Services Division. We set up interviews to determine what specific activities these programs offered. Finally, to answer questions about funding and the relationship of these programs to our nonprofit organization's focus, an interview between teachers and the director of the Youth Center took place.

Creating a visual representation of all the school's programs, activities, and possible interventions allowed teachers and other site leaders to engage in discussions about necessary and unnecessary workloads. At the school, we learned that some of the programs contained "thematic overkill." For instance, students were receiving presentation after presentation, workshop after workshop on life skills from hospital representatives, guest speakers, and program leaders at the Youth Center. We decided to cut down these activities to allow more instructional time throughout the year. While removing these programs would cut possible funding, teachers came up with the idea of creating a "services" hour each week. This hour was carried out by the administration, thus allowing the entire teaching team an hour of release time for collaboration. By the end of its third year, teachers utilized this hour for disaggregating and reporting student data, goal setting, presenting and learning from student work, and other school improvement strategies.

In closing, among the issues of diversifying the student population at the school and providing teachers with more instructional and collaboration time, the staff had the data needed to request an additional staff member from our governing board. The principal was then able to focus the restructuring efforts into efforts aimed at building greater coherence between policy, programs, and resources. An outside consultant was eventually hired to instruct the teaching team on alignment of curriculum with state standards.

The following list details the main issues that needed immediate attention:

- Recruitment of a diverse student body
- Low parental involvement and buy-in to the school's mission and vision
- Handling of students who consistently break the school discipline policy and who, out of fear of losing the average daily attendance (ADA) monies, are given multiple opportunities (services) rather than suspended

- The school's status as a "program" under the umbrella of the nonprofit organization rather than being considered and funded as a distinct and independent entity
- The lack of an agencywide evaluation tool to measure the efficacy of our parent organization's programs and departments

Actions Taken and Results

Teachers did not engage in a comprehensive maneuver; instead we were able to articulate the strategies that best fit to rectify the pressing issues listed above. Focusing on students who negatively influence school culture and on low parental involvement, the staff came up with two solutions:

1. We understood that students not following the school's discipline policies contradicted our high expectations and achievement. We also agreed that these students were usually given a simple slap on the hand and sent back to class. To be fair and judicious, we established a progressive discipline system and explained it to all students and parents: (a) Teachers contacted parents at home before assigning referrals; (b) instances where students were sent to the office with referrals had to be documented; (c) three referrals led to an immediate parent conference; (d) an additional referral meant one-day suspension and a behavior contract thereafter; (e) breaking this contract jeopardized their continuation at the school.

The implementation and consistent execution of this policy soon helped to reduce the number of referrals from 47 to 35 and suspensions from 12 to 8 over the course of one year from the fall semester of 2003 to the spring semester of 2004 (Gómez, 2004, p. 53).

2. We began to organize a monthly parent meeting so that they could communicate with each other. In these meetings parents discussed the needs of their children in relation to the needs of the school. Some parents were given the task of fulfilling a specific role throughout the year, including a "volunteer outreach" coordinator whose task was to call other parents and ask for their assistance during school functions such as dances and cultural celebrations. Perhaps what made the most immediate impact was having parents visit the school once a semester for parent-teacher conferences. These appointments lasted for about 15 minutes, but it was all that was necessary for teachers to finally make the connection between their students and their home lives. In these

conferences, teachers presented parents with their student's grades, behavior report, and social standing. Parents were asked to detail their child's home behavior when it came to school. Before closing the sessions, parents were asked to state how else the school or teaching staff could assist in the academic or social development of their child.

Reflective Questions

- The gray area between being an independent organization and being part of a larger parent organization appears to have limited teachers' leadership in this case. How would you have avoided such a situation?
- What would you say was the real issue behind the lack of a consistent discipline policy?
- How would you use the coherence and mapping tools at your site?

APPLYING THE CONCEPTS IN YOUR WORKPLACE

1. Read the book by Darling-Hammond (1997) and article by Arriaza (2004).

2. Continue and broaden the teacher reflection group. Assure norms and practices of trust so that participants can reflect on and share "how successful various groups of students are being at your school."

3. Use the writings and Reflective and Essential Questions in this chapter to start conversations.

4. Perform an inventory of human and material resources allocation. You can adjust the coherence tool provided below to your specific circumstances.

ESSENTIAL QUESTIONS

1. Which skills account for the effectiveness of teacher leaders in supporting their schools' effort to impact student learning?

2. What would you say are the most effective strategies teacher leaders implement to successfully mobilize institutional and community resources?

RESOURCES

The following is a set of organizing tools developed by G. Arriaza and T. Malarkey (Copyright 2000) to identify coherence issues between resources and community involvement in schools.

Community Connections

The following set of questions needs to be asked around community connections and the school's programs. Use the following questions as guides and map out your findings on the matrix provided below:

- What institutions, organizations, or programs representing or working with the parental and general communities are currently present at the school?
- What kind of activities have these organizations or programs currently set in motion at the school?
- What department, individuals, or programs are involved?
- Who is responsible for what?
- In what ways are these activities integrated, added, or extracurricular to the regular schedule?
- How are these activities funded?
- In what ways are these initiatives connected to the school's focus?

Map A: Support

Institutions, Organizations, Programs	Specific activities	Individuals, departments, programs involved	Sources of funding	Relationship of interventions to the school's focused effort

Respond to the question:

- What coherence exists between the resources invested in the school and the school's focus for the year and its mission? Share the results with the leadership team and faculty.

Map B: School Demographics

Race and Gender Totals		Percentage by Grade		Percentage of Free or Reduced Lunch		Median Family Income		Percentage in Special Education		English Language Development	
Male	Female	Male	Female	Male	Female	Male	Female	Male	Female	Male	Female

Respond to the question:

• What group makes up the majority on what specific area?

76

Community Mapping

A: City Population

Form 3.3 City Population

Race and Ethnicity		Median Annual Income	Employment	Housing	Health
	%				
Totals					

B: City Services

Form 3.4   City Services

Housing	Health	Recreational	Financial	Legal	Youth and Children Programs

C: Community Organizations and Businesses

Form 3.5   Community Organizations and Businesses

Major Community Organizations List	Main Local Business List

Gap Analysis

From your inventory you can then do a gap analysis comparing where you are with where you want to be. The resulting gap can be used as the points of departure for your action plan.

Procedure

1. Have your school's vision and mission at hand.

2. Have your inventory completed and available.

3. Ask first: Where are we? (This question leads to showing what the distribution of resources looks like.)

4. Ask: Where do we want to be? (This question compares the current state of resource distribution with your vision and mission.)

5. List the discrepancy between the current distribution and your vision.

6. Ask: How can we get there? (Identify those gap areas you believe will allow your organization push for the greatest change. Make sure to focus only on these rather than on all and every identified area.)

Gap Analysis Organizer

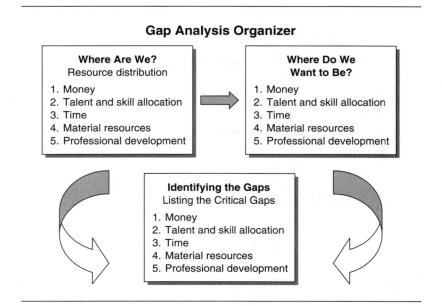

Where Are We?	**Where Do We Want to Be?**
Resource distribution	
1. Money	1. Money
2. Talent and skill allocation	2. Talent and skill allocation
3. Time	3. Time
4. Material resources	4. Material resources
5. Professional development	5. Professional development

Identifying the Gaps
Listing the Critical Gaps

1. Money
2. Talent and skill allocation
3. Time
4. Material resources
5. Professional development

RESOURCES

For technical assistance and information, contact the organizations below and/or any of the teacher leaders listed in this chapter (see Appendix: List of Contributors).

Differentiated instruction

National Center on Accessing the General Curriculum

Contact: www.cast.org/ncac/NCAC362.cfm

Schools Attuned

Contact: www.schoolsattuned.org/

Coalition of Essential Schools

Contact: www.essentialschools.org/

Understanding by Design

UbD resource: www.score.k12.ca.us

UbD resource: http://ubdexchange.org

US Census Bureau

Contact: www.census.gov/

Department of Education

Contact: www.ed.gov/index.jhtml

ENDNOTES

1. French author of *The Little Prince*.

2. *Chunking* is a learning technique or process that allows students to pull out information as they read from manageable amounts of text. Good readers do this automatically, but weaker readers need to be taught to manage the information they take in, analyze it for meaning, and finally combine it with prior knowledge to find relevancy or irrelevancy in it. This technique is important to help construct meaning of text; retention of information is central to strong comprehension.

3. *Subvocalizing* is a learning strategy that asks a student to verbalize aloud with someone else or simply themselves after reading

text. This can be done as a group rehearsal as well. Students picture in their minds the words and ideas as they vocalize to tap into both the visual cues and verbal cues from which they might benefit. For students who learn best orally (i.e., receptive language), this is a means to utilize a strong modality to support a weaker one (i.e., expressive language).

4. Levine's Schools Attuned program is a professional development program that helps educators acquire knowledge and skills and offers a system of tools to meet the diverse learning needs of students. It is a program that equips teachers to make the best instructional decisions to ensure that each student finds academic and social success in some way. Actually, it's a program about good teaching practices for all.

5. *Graphomotor* skills are those skills we use when we use a pencil or pen. These skills are not the same as fine motor skills. In fact, the muscles used to write are different from those used, for example, to sew, knit, or build.

6. The school's vision statement reads: "Our mission is to empower students to excel personally, to succeed in college, and to flourish and lead in a diverse world to create positive change" (Macsa Academia Calmecac Charter, 2000, p. 4).

CHAPTER FOUR

The Role of Inquiry

Enduring Understandings

- Skillful leaders generate their own knowledge base in order to make informed decisions about their practices and their institution's policies.
- Skillful leaders also use professional knowledge to inform their practice.
- A culture of inquiry implies changes in teachers' daily talk and in how they examine student work and their own work.

Adopting an inquiry stance invites a teacher to seek connection with students and to look at their learning challenges as fascinating and important puzzles. Connection opens the heart and mind to new possibilities and these sorts of puzzles.

(Radin, 2004, p. 78)

Until we begin to routinely respect and respond to the best that is known about effective teaching and organizational improvement, we forfeit the benefits of the rich knowledge base that can inform our teamwork as we pursue substantive goals. Until we routinely consult this knowledge base, we limit every student and teacher in our system.

(Schmoker, 1996, p. 65)

C reating homegrown knowledge is nothing new to teachers. For as long as mass education has existed, teachers have learned from each other's experiences through informal conversations, staff development activities, professional conferences, lectures by experts, and formal teacher preparation and graduate programs offered by colleges of education (Tyack, 1974). These types of services provided to teachers characterize much of their professional development experience. One feature remains constant throughout this inservice approach: Experts legitimize teachers' knowledge. In the last 20 years, quality professional development, slowly but consistently, has shifted to being tied to the legitimization of locally generated knowledge by teachers themselves, using this knowledge for reforming schools and informing practice (Fullan, 1991) and redefining teacher learning as a lifelong endeavor.

Knowledge produced by and for *teachers as researchers* and as *evidence-based leaders* is a relatively new area of the teaching profession. Traditionally, university researchers have done this job through typical armchair research projects. This kind of study follows a traditional cycle: Formulate the inquiry; define the research model and method; and then launch the study in schools and school districts and write and publish the findings. In this research approach, universities function at the giving end of knowledge and schools at the receiving end. Thus, teachers and students serve as objects of study rather than subjects able to create systematic knowledge out of their daily experience. For decades, this tradition has split the field of education into those who research and those being researched. It is not surprising that throughout the last century, most scholarship on schools offers an outsider, third-person perspective. As a result, this approach has cast teachers as practitioners and researchers as knowledge producers, in other words, teachers as "the doers" and researchers as "the thinkers." In reality, this model rendered the knowledge thus produced of limited relevance to teachers and therefore of little lasting impact on classroom practice.

As the definition of school leadership has changed, skillful school leaders increasingly use evidence generated at the site and district levels for decision making. Schools gather and use data, not only to comply with legal state and federal mandates but to monitor students' academic progress, identify and calibrate teaching practices, and inform curricular and policy decisions. Indeed, looking at the results of one's labor opens a world of intriguing questions, whets the appetite for knowledge, and widens the space for creativity. Teacher leaders engage in collaborative action research, using qualitative and quantitative data, as a strategy to better accomplish their work. One result is that teachers come to view themselves and their peers in a more professional way.

What do we mean by this methodology? In this chapter, we first offer the definition and procedures of collaborative action research and then illustrate its application through three samples: First we look at the team dynamics of inquiry as a collaborative endeavor and the value of dissenting voices; second, we delve into the impact of teacher inquiry on classroom work; third, we describe the application of inquiry to a whole school. Above all, these stories are both about the human scale of cultural and systemic change in schools and of change conceived for the long haul.

DEFINITION OF COLLABORATIVE ACTION RESEARCH

We understand collaborative action research as an iterative, mixed-methods approach to research (see Sagor, 2004). It is collaborative in the sense that teachers work in teams and involve their school's faculty in the process. In addition, the school administration and, in many cases, the district office often participate. Teamwork functions as a key checks-and-balances mechanism against bias and against cynicism. Teachers as researchers keep each other honest both around the authenticity of the evidence being used and about its interpretation.

The action side of this methodology builds on the long tradition of applied research, one that is concerned with the improvement of the life and work circumstances of the participating institution. Teachers seek understanding of the challenges they face in the classroom and/or the school as a whole; they define and apply solutions to those challenges and examine the results. In other words, inquiry is always tied to understanding the results of one's actions.

Collaborative action research requires data systems that supply timely information. Systematized and up-to-date data make it possible for teachers to know the effects of programs, multiple assessments, discipline, and other school climate issues. Data systems must be user friendly, easily retrievable, and available all the time. From asking empirical questions about concrete classroom level practices to larger schoolwide concerns, collaborative action research is, ultimately, a *habit of mind* that helps to build a supportive school culture.

This inquiry follows a logical, systematic process that requires from teachers not only intellectual discipline but also the skill to involve the entire organization. Thus, inquiry follows a cycle and a way of talking. This cycle is always anchored on the school's focus and vision. Teachers thoroughly examine multiple sources of academic performance (e.g., test scores, projects, portfolios) and social relations (e.g., friendship groups, working groups, individual social status) to uncover the root causes of unacceptable academic performance and inequities. This cycle can follow these steps:

1. Examining data to identify the problems affecting equity and academic excellence

2. Formulating an empirical question(s) one believes will yield the best discoveries and explanations to the identified problem

3. Reviewing at different moments throughout the cycle what research tells about the problem under study

4. Selecting a possible solution

5. Mobilizing organizational and community support to address the problem

6. Implementing the possible solution

7. Collecting data generated by the action and examining the results

8. Disseminating the learning

9. Going back again to step one: examining the new evidence as to how the identified problem has been affected by the applied solution. At this point, it might be necessary to formulate new empirical question(s) and to initiate a new cycle. These cycles always go back to the same beginning, but moving upward in a spiral fashion—the same departure but at a higher vantage point.

This cycle of inquiry is shown in Figure 4.1.

Talking about evidence requires that teacher leaders acquire and practice a set of skills to ensure that (a) nobody is left out of the process, (b) the staff embraces it as their own, (c) understanding grows naturally out of a collective effort, and (d) while accounting for one's work, it is for learning purposes, not for punishment. For a process of this kind to happen, teacher leaders make sure to remove blame from the conversation and make sure to eliminate avoidance. When these behaviors are continuously practiced, it is assumed that a culture of trust and respect emerges.

Facilitating data talks follows a protocol that when applied carefully allows staff to explore the challenges at hand in constructive ways:

1. Read only what the data tell (i.e., do not jump to conclusions and solutions).

2. Identify the problems over which the staff has some control (i.e., within the confines of the school).

3. Take on the problems whose solutions are most doable (i.e., data sources are accessible, expertise is within reach).

Figure 4.1   Cycle of Inquiry

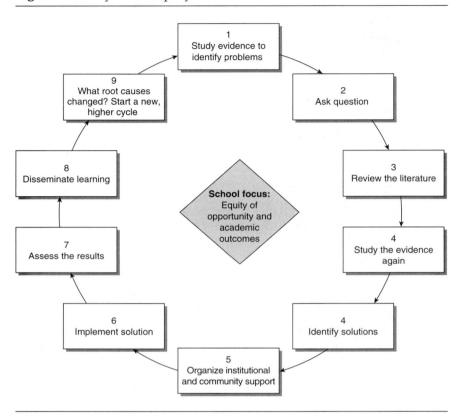

4. Follow systematically a cycle of inquiry (i.e., like the one in Figure 4.1).

From Schmoker's quasi-admonition (quoted at the head of this chapter) to today, about 10 years have passed. Collaborative action research promises to reconfigure schools into intelligent spaces where traditionally private practice is transformed into public, where learning fertilizes ordinary conversation, where new realities are created on solid empirical evidence, and an evidence-based leadership flourishes. Aided by computer technology for collecting and analyzing student data, today's new kind of educational leaders increasingly infuse data and inquiry into the life of their schools, and systematic knowledge production by and for teachers is validated. Programs and concrete interventions no longer are simply launched and left to perish in oblivion. In our view, systematic inquiry implies a cultural shift. The following three narratives illustrate these points.

COLLABORATIVE ACTION RESEARCH, WHEN WELL CONDUCTED, BRINGS OUT THE BEST IN ITS MEMBERS

Collaborative action instills a sense of group effort, opens the conversation, and definitely generates deep and respectful professional relations. Team members speak up, propose ideas without hesitation, and bring to bear their skills and expertise without restrictions. Helena Lebedeff Bradford, Robert Hatcher, Kristin Pfotenhauer-Sharp, Nancy Migdall, and Jennifer Schmidt teamed up across subject matter, functions, and seniority.

> Often those who resist have something important to tell us. People resist for what they view as good reasons. They may see alternatives we never dreamed of. They may understand problems about the minutiae of implementation that we never see from our lofty perch atop Mount Olympus. (Maurer, in Fullan, 2000, p. 159)

Our action research began with an uncomfortable month in which we were identifying our problem and process and Robert kept expressing doubt about the identified problem and methodology.

At one point, Robert began to question his frustrations and asked Jennifer for input before initiating a series of e-mails. He stated in a note of March 15, 2003: "I delayed sending and checked with Jennifer to see if I am totally off base, or just being me, or both."

His multiple concerns included these:

- The pre- and posttests, particularly with our targeted population
- The targeted population for this experiment
- Causation and validity

- Teacher participation
- The time
- And the race vs. class issue

A week later, Robert added, "The more I look at this, the more frustrated I become. It is the timeline and the size of the job. . . . Wish I understood the answers."

Robert's questions created a tension within the group. The methodology was due, we had collaborated in Robert's absence to refine our problem statement, and now Robert was bringing up these major questions and concerns. The group was torn between dismissing his concerns so that we could get it done and trying to clarify what seemed crystal clear. We were researching the literature looking for studies and theories on our topic, and Robert was putting the brakes on. During our weekly meetings, Robert would ask for clarification regarding some aspect of the action research. We would discuss this and then make the assumption that we were clear and ready to progress. It wasn't until Robert wrote an extensive e-mail outlining his concerns that we became aware of how far-reaching his concerns were.

Our frustrations increased as we tried to clarify the topic and methodology for the action research. We would believe the scope of our project was clear, and Robert would ask yet another irritating question and confuse us all or cause us to repeat an earlier discussion. Finally, at the brink of total frustration, Nancy asked, "Robert, *what* is so hard to *understand?* We are trying to provide literacy support to kids who didn't pass the High School Exit Exam." At this point, recognizing Robert's concerns were not going away, we asked Robert to clarify his frustrations.

As we listened to his argument, it became clear to us that Robert continued to build on his previous concerns. His remarks included the following:

- The apparent untidiness of the research project. Would we have enough data to make any conclusions?
- If we were working with students who had not passed the California High School Exit Exam (CAHSEE), would we have the results back to know if they improved in time for the due date of the project?
- There was no clear control group.

Listening to Robert led to a meaningful discussion that clarified the value of action research as an ongoing project beyond the scope of the San Jose State University graduate program. The project was giving us the skills to collect, study, and interpret data for future action research.

To establish a clear control group, Kristin suggested comparing the first semester academic literacy students with those enrolled in the second semester section and to compare the students enrolled in the Composition and Literacy class with the English Language Learners (ELL) group who did not have English Language Development (ELD) support. It was also suggested that our continued bibliography research might lead to some specific literacy strategies we could later use. This satisfied Robert, and we realized that the action research project didn't necessarily have to be solved by the project's due date and have all the answers. The value of the action research process was what became clear and important.

Together we agreed that research is research regardless of the results. Knowing what not to repeat was worth knowing. Results would be based on the data we did have—but we could follow up with more data later. Regardless of the outcome, we still would have gathered multiple excellent literacy strategies that we would later share with staff and implement in our own classes, as well as in the Academic Literacy class.

Working through these frustrations helped us clarify what we were doing, and thus we were able to concentrate on all of the vagaries of literacy strategies and their role in improving student achievement. We had a better defined action research project with an explicit purpose and a scientifically sound process. We were also better able to talk honestly with each other and have yet to encounter another dilemma that impedes our process as a result of improved communication.

The experience made us realize that if we were running through all of these problems with someone who was ostensibly with us in the process, how much more difficult would it be if the questions were from someone who wasn't invested in the problem. As teachers, we know that we don't check for understanding by saying, "Got it? OK. Let's move on." If we had built a protocol into our meetings to elicit from everybody their version of our work together, we could have prevented the tension that resulted when Robert's frustrations weren't clearly addressed for him.

As Chaleff writes in *The Courageous Follower* (1995), "The pain of the breakdown serves the function of demanding that we pay attention to our need to change" (p. 127).

Luckily, the world has its Roberts.

Reflective Questions

- What does listening have to do with teamwork?
- How would you characterize the strategies this team used to address open resistance?
- Why was it so important to the team to build cohesion?
- What do you take as lessons to your school?

ACTION RESEARCH HAS AN INVALUABLE APPLICATION TO THE CLASSROOM

Skillful teacher leaders apply action research to classroom practice with the school as a whole in mind. Kimberly Marion, Laurie Belanger, Lori Gaines, and Nirmala George launched an inquiry honing in on classroom practices. Their goal was to change the conversation about students' academic performance by making collaboration a centerpiece of teachers' work.

The need to initiate a shift in the conversation among teachers through collaboration arose from two facts. As a team, we observed that when students were switching one class for another, they were leaving with different levels of content knowledge. It was obvious to us that these discontinuities should not exist in a program if teachers work together to agree on and follow a certain format and routine throughout the year. Collaboration time, we thought, is a time for teachers to work together to further students' achievement and success. It is to be used for a variety of activities, including designing common assessments, integrating curriculum, and looking at student work and data, to name a few. Thus, we speculated that teacher collaboration could give us the most powerful lever to help change discontinuities, since the school had already allocated a weekly "collaboration time" that seemed unused.

Teacher collaboration at our school has indeed been a challenge for a long time. We have scheduled time to work together across grade levels and subject matter on a permanent basis, but our team's observations and experience saw a lack of effective collaboration around teaching practices, assessments, and students' academic performance across all departments. Teachers had the time and used it for purposes other than working as collaborators. We wanted to change such a dysfunctional system, ultimately as a way to enhance students' academic performance.

For five years, the school has been focusing on "narrowing the gap" between African American and Latino students, on one hand, and Caucasian and Asian students on the other. Over this time, the school has focused on literacy and personalization as two overriding strategies. Teachers have made some strides toward personalization, particularly through the creation of academies.

We had two assumptions:

1. By focusing the conversation among teachers on covered common curriculum, students would be able to pick up where they left off in the previous class and follow through the rest of the semester without difficulty in another class.

2. Collaboration around the creation and use of common end-of-semester assessments would help drive consistency in instruction, as well as improve students' academic success.

Methodology

We selected teachers from the subjects and departments in which our team members were already involved (English II, Spanish I, Geometry, and Biology) and followed them through two semesters, although data for the study covered two years (2002–2003 and 2003–2004). We created four collaborative teams, one per subject. The fact that each of us worked in these programs made it less difficult to find interested colleagues to be part of a collaboration that would design end-of-semester exit exams and monitor that the state standards were followed in all classes. The school principal was fully in support of our efforts, but no actual administrative interventions were required.

We designed a preassessment to gauge students' knowledge and skill prior to starting the semester. Using these instruments across our four subjects would allow us to then measure growth and identify consistencies.

We established as a requisite that students who moved from one section to another would be exposed to the same standards and curriculum during the same period of time.

Besides our active involvement in each of the four collaborative groups, we documented the work through a survey administrated twice: spring of 2003 and spring of 2004 and formal and informal interviews with participating teachers.

Results

1. Working together to design a standards-based common assessment in general led to an increase in collaboration among participating teachers in all four programs.

2. There was a 12% drop in the number of teachers who observed a discrepancy in what they had covered and what students transferring into their classes had covered.

3. Students in Geometry improved their GPA from 2.04 in 2003 to 2.26 in 2004. We observed, however, a drop of about one quarter of a point during the same period in Biology, about one tenth of a point in English II, and about one fifth of a point in Spanish I.

4. Students also met almost all state academic standards in all courses.

Conclusions and Recommendations

Action research has promoted collaboration around concrete projects that have direct benefits to all participants. Some teachers, English teachers particularly, found it difficult to let go of some of the autonomy in order to give a common assessment. Yet as a solution, they developed common rubrics that can be implemented regardless of the materials used.

Through this collaboration, it became clear to Geometry teachers that the standards they thought were important during the first year of the study were not the ones they ended up focusing on, which in turn affected the number of standards met.

Two recommendations:

- Keep structured time for collaboration. Not only does collaboration help in self-reflection, it helps to see what is working in other classrooms.
- Increase student expectations by working on the standards. While Biology students and English students met all of the standards the first semester, in the other two programs students did not. Meeting the standards, to a large extent, leads to achieving our own expectations.

Reflective Questions

- What were the key obstacles in the way of using time for teacher collaboration?
- The team's theory of action was that teachers would change by finding collaboration a meaningful activity only if the time spent together around inquiry impacted their own learning and that of their students. Do you think the team succeeded? Why? Why not?
- In what ways did the team help departments to gather data and to disseminate information?
- What is in this story for you?

THE POTENTIAL POWER OF COLLABORATIVE ACTION RESEARCH AS A METHODOLOGY TO ENACT SCHOOLWIDE SUSTAINED CHANGE

Melissa Sherman, Jason Viloria, Felicia Webb, and Hannah MacKinnon engaged in action research aimed at assessing the impact a curriculum dealing with college-going expectations would have on the student population. The inquiry led these teachers to work with agencies outside the school, as well as with school administration. The project became a schoolwide activity and was shared with the other high schools in the district. The team presented their findings to the school board, and the team's curriculum has now been adopted by the district.

Our school was founded in 1976 on the concept of small learning communities. It began as three small schools within a large school. The school mission statement during those first years read, "Everyone is someone special." Students were assigned a homeroom teacher who tracked their progress for their three-year high school experience—tenth to twelfth grades—providing academic guidance, study skills, as well as college information. The small-school emphasis faded over time, and the school is now a typical comprehensive high school. The staff consists of 45 teachers, 4 administrators, and a cast of support staff, all constantly battling turnover. The student body (over 2,650) is 51% Latino, 11% African American, 19% White, 13% Asian, and the remainder a mixture of Pacific Islander and American Indian.

In the past seven years, our school has seen a dramatic decline in the number of students going to two-year and four-year colleges. In 1996, about 64% of our graduates attended college immediately after high school. This number had declined to 53% in 2002. Our school district has made attempts to increase the college-going rates of all students by increasing the graduation requirements from 220 credits to 240 credits. This increased the number of graduating seniors meeting the prerequisites for the California public universities from 21% in 2000–2001 to 53% in 2001–2002. Although more students are graduating as university eligible, there has not been an increase in the actual number of students attending college.

We decided to focus our action research project on creating a stronger college-going culture at our school. The team was aided in the effort by the GEAR UP project from San Jose State University (see the Resources section at end of this chapter).

The need for college/career awareness prompted us to lead in the development of districtwide college/career standards for grades 9–12. We spent the summer of 2003 working with GEAR UP staff in creating a comprehensive college/career awareness curriculum to meet such standards. The curriculum attempted to improve three areas: (a) students' expectations, (b) knowledge of colleges and career materials, and (c) overall college-going rates. As we made plans to create the curriculum, it became apparent that nothing like what we were planning on doing previously existed at the school or district level, and implementing it into every grade level seemed quite challenging. We started building from the ninth grade up. We organized the curriculum around themes for each grade level. Thus ninth grade became "Knowing Who You Are"; tenth grade—"Discovering the Right Path"; eleventh grade—"Got Career?"; and twelfth grade—"Dreams to Reality." We designed the work around three areas: vocabulary, goal setting, and engaging lessons.

Since the school did not have a college/career technician, there was no one besides us to help implement the curriculum. We felt a bit lost as to how to be supportive to the teachers who were teaching the curriculum, as well as how to ensure its actual delivery. Most interactions with our peers were through e-mail and one-on-one conversation. Thus very little accountability existed among the staff. Administrators were supportive of our work by giving us time to speak with those willing to meet with us and, whenever we needed, supplying us with data. Administrators weren't sure what their roles were in providing momentum toward teaching the curriculum. It was difficult negotiating our relations with our colleagues in the implementation phase. Our team worked hard in maintaining solid relationships with fellow teachers, for we knew that since it was the curriculum's pilot year, our colleagues teaching it were, in a way, doing us a favor. Nonetheless, the team was unable to get all teachers to deliver the curriculum.

As the curriculum grew, so did the efforts of GEAR UP and the district superintendent, who now wanted all schools to adopt a similar curriculum. Our team presented the work at a GEAR UP conference in San Diego at some of the other high schools in our district, and to the school board.

The relationship of college or career awareness to students' own expectations was the area of greatest concern for us; after piloting the curriculum, we saw clear gains. It became evident that, while most students had set high expectations for themselves prior to the implementation of the curriculum, they lacked the general knowledge regarding how to achieve those goals.

Those of us who worked on the implementation and follow-up of this curriculum demonstrated the tremendous potential of a curriculum that attempts to shift a culture of low expectations and mediocrity into one of high expectations and excellence. When teachers agree and understand the value of a coherent, schoolwide, sequential curriculum that focuses on building students' expectations, skills, and knowledge about college and career awareness, we can observe a cultural change that translates to increasing the life chances of our youth. And for that to happen, teachers, administrators, and the district office need to work together.

Reflective Questions

- Having a well-focused issue is a key concern to the team's action research. What cultural ramifications can you identify as a result of such a focus?
- How important was the collaboration with district and school administration and the role played by important allies (e.g., GEAR UP)?
- What do you need to do to integrate action research at your site?

APPLYING THE CONCEPTS IN YOUR WORKPLACE

1. Read *The Action Research Guidebook: A Four-Step Process for Educators and School Teams* by Richard Sagor (2004) and *The Results Fieldbook: Practical Strategies From Dramatically Improved Schools* by Mike Schmoker (2001).

2. Continue and broaden the teacher reflection group. Assure norms and practices of trust so that participants can reflect on and share *how they use inquiry to inform their practice.*

3. Use the writings and Reflective and Essential Questions in this chapter to start conversations.

4. Initiate your own inquiry. If at your site no inquiry tradition exists, start from the beginning. If there is a tradition of inquiry, then go to item (c).
   (a) Identify two other colleagues who share your concerns and interest. They could be teachers teaching the same students, subject, or grade level.
   (b) Norm the conversation. From the outset make sure to agree on the terms of the relationship and what norms will ground your conversation (see this chapter's first section, Definition of Collaborative Action Research).

(c) Select no less than three pieces of evidence to corroborate what they say about the same issue you are investigating.

(d) Dig a little deeper into possible explanations as to the reasons the evidence shows the academic performance you see. Tools such as the Five Whys can be handy (see Resources below).

(e) Initiate your cycle of inquiry (see steps in this chapter's first section, Definition of Collaborative Action Research, Figure 4.1).

(f) Make sure the school administration allocates time and resources for your inquiry.

(g) Have a dissemination plan in coordination with the school administration so that your experience is replicated by others at the site.

ESSENTIAL QUESTIONS

1. In what ways does local knowledge and knowledge produced by outside experts productively impact teaching and learning at your school?

2. What cultural practices do schools need in order to support collaborative action research?

3. How can action research inform your school community to promote policies and practices that support maximizing learning of all students?

RESOURCES

GEAR UP (Gaining Early Awareness and Readiness for Undergraduate Programs) is a federally funded support program for high school students. Contact at the federal government's office:

www.ed.gov/programs/gearup/gu-fy1999-part-grantees. html

Contact in San Jose State University:

www.sjsu.edu/counselored/gearup

Dr. Xiaolu Hu 408–924–3668

The Five Whys

This is a modified tool based on the original created by Peter Senge (2000). The tool is suggested as one way to identify possible causal relations of academic performance or social interaction.

- Step one: Agree with your team on a piece of data that highlights your concern (e.g., English Language Learners reading scores; the number of male students being reported for unacceptable behavior).
- Step two: Based on the selected data, formulate a statement describing what the challenge is. Use active verbs in a direct and simple sentence.
- Step three: Select one of the statements. Choose the one statement you believe might offer the greatest leverage for change.
- Step four: Brainstorm as to WHY you think you are having such an issue. Make sure that the answers begin with BECAUSE. Depending on the team's size, go over this first WHY one time per member and repeat until you exhaust possible BECAUSES.
- Step five: Now go back to step three. Repeat this process at least five times.
  1. At the end you will have a statement as to the possible cause of an issue you want to research.
  2. Change the statement into a researchable question.
  3. Anchor your question on the school and/or district's vision.
  4. Initiate your cycle of inquiry (see this chapter's first section, Definition of Collaborative Action Research, Figure 4.1).

CHAPTER FIVE

Building Equity in Diverse Classrooms

> ### Enduring Understandings
>
> - Students learn best in schools in which they are honored and respected for the assets they bring to the school.
> - Equity is about doing whatever it takes to personalize the daily experience of all and every student.
> - In schools in which all students are supported to maximize their learning, skillful, collaborative teacher leadership focuses professional development, resources, and conversation on issues of equity and pedagogy.

Getting to know students doesn't happen all at once. It builds over time, through paying attention to what individual students say and do—and don't—in the classroom and the hallways, and in their written work, speech patterns and physical appearance.

(Cushman, 2003, pp. 3–4)

Equity measures—or extra measures—must be taken in order to bring about the desired goals of fairness, same status and at least the same academic outcomes among students of color as found among White students as a group. . . . The spirit of equity is at the heart of all gap-closing measures since inequity is being acknowledged if equity is being discussed.

(Lee, 1996, p. 33)

In our society, schools are called upon to play a pivotal role in forging a well-informed and educated citizenry. *All* students must be expected and supported to use their minds and hearts well. Schools must therefore create equitable conditions that remove the roadblocks that make it so difficult for certain groups of students to meet these expectations.

In our view, democracy is grounded on equitable social and economic relations. Many, including Thomas Jefferson, have said that this type of citizenry is the best guard against tyranny and the most potent sustenance of freedom and, ultimately, of a regime of the people for the people. This assertion explains, in a way, the open and locally controlled public education system of this country. It is not strange, therefore, that the institution of schooling has, since its inception, been a contested terrain between those who believe in the noble twin principles of democracy and equity and those who push for the opposite—schools as a place to perpetuate the privileges of the few.

Teacher leadership is, above all, about equity. Equity, we propose, is a tenet and a habit. It is not part of a political philosophy or simply an ideological item. Equity is a principle and a way of being that has to do with how we as educators make the institution of schooling fulfill the commitment to educate every single child regardless of race, class, gender, physical challenges, sexual orientation, language, and other circumstances. Skillful teacher leaders see everything that takes place in schools through the understanding that their job is to forge citizens who use their minds and hearts well. The point of departure for this understanding is a simple one: the unequivocal rejection of deficit models and respect for the assets all students bring to school. *Assets* means here the "funds" of knowledge (cultural richness, linguistic diversity, and diversity of experience) embedded in the lives of each and all students and their families. These assets constitute a source of power and the potential for positive transformation. In order to produce equitable academic outcomes, educators and leaders must do whatever is needed to level off the inequities students come to the school with, which are rooted in a hierarchically structured society.

Equity in schools is about full access to the sources and means of knowledge, skill, and understanding. Schools are institutions that can enable children to remove social, cultural, and institutional barriers and thus increase their life chances. Regardless of background factors, schools *do* and *can* equip children with the knowledge, understanding, skills, and habits of mind and heart to contribute to the welfare of society and this way to the pursuit of their full potential, their own happiness, and the sustainability of a democratic society. Schools must foster the resiliency of each and every child!

The two most critical issues teacher leaders encounter in their attempt to enact equity are (a) how to advance equity outcomes without creating new inequities and (b) how to know whether the school is succeeding in its equity efforts. We, therefore, posit that three spheres of action form the axis of leading for equity. One sphere is the distribution of work according to students' needs and challenges; the second is about personalizing teaching and learning; and the third is about having students' academic performance at the center of staff conversations. The following sections illustrate how teacher leaders address these spheres.

DISTRIBUTING TEACHERS' WORK

Distributing the human talent, money, material resources, and time available to address the challenges of every single child and group—in ways in which academic achievement continually increases for all students—entails a tremendous individual and institutional effort. It is so because one confronts long established practices that often protect and hide privilege and entitlements. Teachers leading for equity promote collegial collaboration around teaching and learning. In their schools, teacher leaders make pedagogical decisions based on empirical evidence and ongoing inquiry. Of all these work areas, assigning teachers to work with students lagging behind in their academic preparation is perhaps the most difficult task to take on.

Laurie Belanger, a high school science teacher, takes us through her own professional journey. She tells what leading for the sake of equitable distribution of labor and serving students well has meant for her.

During my first year of teaching grades 9–10, I was in three different rooms teaching three different classes. I was then still going to school, trying to finish my credential, writing lesson plans into the wee hours of the night, and dealing with classroom management issues that college definitely had not prepared me for—as in "How do I deal with students constantly in my face and refusing to do anything?" I was distraught every day, even crying, because I didn't think I was giving the kids what they deserved. I just didn't have enough experience.

While the other teachers in the science department tried to console me, they definitely wouldn't have taken on my teaching assignments. They had already "paid their dues," as the saying goes, and it was the newbie's turn. Everyone, including administrators, agreed that someone with more experience would better serve the toughest kids, but no one was willing to change the way things are done. I was at that school for one semester, and then I headed for what I hoped would be a better teaching situation. By then I knew I could not survive as a teacher if I didn't leave.

My second teaching job was at the high school where I once had been a student. It didn't really start out any better for me at my new site. One other teacher and I were hired into the Science Department in 1999, and we both started out the year teaching science in the library because there were no actual classrooms for us. While I only had two preparations, I had three classes of Integrated Science that posed some definite classroom management issues. Not only was I dealing with honing my management skills, I also had to find a way to make science fun in a facility that couldn't have been less like a science classroom. It was trial by fire, but fortunately my previous teaching experience helped me survive that first year.

I always said back then that if I was ever the one to make decisions regarding teaching assignments, I would assign the veteran teachers to the more challenging classes. Doesn't it only make sense to have the teachers with more experience teaching the classes with the tougher classroom management issues? This would mean that those experienced teachers would take on the freshmen or SDAIE level classes (Specially Designed Academic Instruction in English); and when ideal facilities are not available, it should be the veteran teachers who take on that added burden and definitely not first-year, inexperienced teachers. The problem is that there is a *system*, and the new teachers get the worst teaching assignments, as I did. In this inequitable system, a teacher, after being at the school for a few years, can "earn" his or her way into upper level classes.

Then an opportunity opened up: The AP Biology program was in need of a new teacher. I jumped at the chance. I would be teaching AP Biology and Biology and working with upperclassmen with none of the discipline issues I once had. The retiring teacher had taught this schedule for 20 years, and I was locked in. Lucky me! I had taken my turn with Integrated Science; now it was someone else's time.

Later, when the Science Department lead teacher became an administrator and left, the Science Department signed a petition and sent it to the principal saying that they wanted me to be their new lead. I interviewed with the principal, and although he had some reservations about having a new teacher become the lead of the Science Department, he knew I had the backing of the staff.

Now, I thought, I'd change that old inequitable system at the school. I was, however, questioned by veteran teachers who argued that they had taken on the toughest classes when they were new. I understood where they were coming from, and I wondered whether they had or hadn't earned the right to teach classes without having to worry about kids who still needed to learn how to act properly in class.

As the new department lead, I had to come up with the teaching assignments and schedule for the next year. We had six new teachers joining our department and an entry level English Language Development (ELD) class that needed a teacher. Veterans in the department were adamant about a brand new teacher getting the class. Again I was pressed by the same old question—How could a teacher with no experience teach a class of kids who spoke no English and deal with tough classroom management issues? Of course, I knew the answer: No one new could. Hence someone with experience would have to take this class.

The other issue I encountered was Integrated Science, a freshmen course for the students who are not yet ready to take Biology. No one left in the department wanted to teach this course either, which meant the new teachers would be assigned to it. Unfortunately, being in my first year as department lead and taking on a class I had never taught, I caved. I gave two new teachers four sections of

Integrated Science apiece. By the end of the year, one of those teachers had left for another school district. The teacher who left was frustrated with the lack of support from both administration and our new teacher program. I did, however, give an ELD class to a veteran, who, because of the culture of the school, took that as an insult and did nothing but show videos for the entire year. Though I tried to intervene, the teacher was set in his ways and wouldn't budge, even with prodding from administration. Luckily, the administration worked hard and found someone with experience teaching ELD for this class the following year. The unfortunate part is that there were no consequences for a teacher's blatantly doing a poor job. The administration does not like to ruffle feathers, especially those of a veteran teacher who would fight back with tooth and nail.

What was I going to do for the following year? I had to come up with another strategy for teaching assignments. I decided that the teachers of the department needed to physically see the distribution of classes and to have a say in what happened in the department. I put everybody's name on a separate piece of butcher paper and hung them up; I put each class section for the department on a slip of paper and had the teachers build their own schedules. Keep in mind we had one piece of butcher paper for the teacher who left and whose replacement needed a schedule. Everyone built his or her own schedule, and what was left for the new teacher were five sections of Integrated Science, a schedule that I wouldn't wish on anybody. We looked at that person's schedule as a department, and after much discussion and argument, the new person ended up with four sections of Integrated Science and one section of Biology. This was still an extremely challenging schedule for a new teacher, but I was unwilling to go against the department and be the leader that I should have been.

After teaching for a little over a semester, the new teacher had nothing but problems. Everyone was sympathetic and tried to help, but the attitude of the department was that she's new and needs to pay her dues. I hoped that she would be back next year!

Then finally I came to the realization that when it comes to teaching assignments, I need to lead by example; that is, unless I'm willing to take on the tougher classes, I can't expect anyone else to. Oh yes, we had the discussion about equity at our department meetings—not only for students but also teachers—but somehow no one was willing to step up to the plate.

Therefore, the first thing I did was to solicit a new teacher to replace me for AP Biology. This is an upper level class that while challenging to teach, does not pose the same problems with management. No one wanted to take on the work that an AP class entails—so I concluded I'd keep it. I then sent around a draft of a class schedule for next year with all teaching assignments evenly distributed. *No one* would be teaching more than two sections of Integrated Science. On this schedule, I have myself teaching two sections of the "dreaded" Integrated Science. Significantly, I have heard no complaints from teachers so far.

All of us scheduled to teach Integrated Science are talking together, and I've expressed my excitement about taking on the challenge. We have a new textbook with new curriculum, so this will be a completely new class for us. We have all admitted to a bit of nervousness; for many of us it's been a few years since we've had to deal with any major discipline issues. I have brought up the idea of collaborating on lesson plans and assessments as I did with the Biology teachers last year. Everyone seems excited about it. Miraculously, teachers who yelled at me last year because they had to teach one section now seem eager to work together in the upcoming year.

I needed to lead by example and show that I'm ready to buy into what I've been trying to sell, that the more experienced should be taking on the tougher classes. Only with an experienced teacher will the students who really need support get what they should out of a class.

Reflective Questions

- How similar or different were the first years of Ms. Belanger at the two schools?
- "Paying one's dues" seems to be a quite prevalent practice in many schools. Which departments or grades at your site continue with this practice?
- What would you argue is motivating Ms. Belanger to "lead by example"?
- What else is in Ms. Belanger's experience that speaks to your own experience?
- What do you think are the underlying issues in Ms. Belanger's concern with tough classroom management approaches and English Language Learners?

Personalizing Teaching and Learning

Knowing students well is both a precondition and a result of a culture that engenders equity outcomes. This process begins with teachers knowing themselves well. Teacher leaders examine their positioning in society from the privileges and disadvantages inscribed in their race, ethnicity, gender, socioeconomics, sexual orientation, and other crucial sociocultural markers. A clear and uncompromising position as to who one is as a social agent provides an extremely important edge to one's work. Knowing where one stands on issues, what one's prejudices are made of, and what one's capacity to effect positive change is provides the foundation for social action. Teacher leaders sustain this self-critical stance by working collaboratively with others and conceive this metacognitive skill as a habit rather than as a temporary task. Thus, teacher leaders engage personal prejudices constantly and facilitate such examination with staff on an ongoing basis. Teacher leaders certainly believe that this habit is a lifelong commitment and an ever enriching journey of self-discovery. Knowing oneself is the springboard to knowing students.

Four sources have dramatically contributed to the understanding of the linkages between knowing students well and equity: (a) educating children with learning and/or physical challenges; (b) providing language development to non- and limited-English speakers; (c) integrating multicultural perspectives in the content areas; and (d) recent advances in neuroscience research, cognitive science, and developmental psychology theories. All of these sources have triggered new and insightful understandings on how learning occurs and the ways to assess it. Tailoring curriculum and delivery systems to the specific circumstances of individual students and groups constitutes one part of teacher leaders' self-defined job description. As a result, countless schools have, over the last 20 years, increased their capacity to address learning challenges in ways never seen before.

Kathleen Cushman, as we quoted her at the top of this chapter, reminds us how simple the process of knowing students well is. It does take time, and above all, Cushman tells, it is achieved through constant observation and active listening, from paying attention to what and how individuals (and groups) express themselves. Knowing all students well is, in other words, the only avenue to distinguishing their potential and needs, and it is the surest way to identify appropriate learning strategies. This is teachers' first professional act. Once this is done well, everything else falls into place, from classroom practices to curriculum planning.

Differentiating instruction means organizing the subject matter and assessing what students know and are capable of doing, with one clear goal in mind: elevating their knowledge, understanding, skills, and habits so as to increase their life chances. Differentiating instruction means that teachers use inquiry to identify students' specific needs and challenges and involve the whole community in the process. The following two stories illustrate how teacher leaders develop the capacity to know the specific needs of their students and colleagues. Emily Lino Diaz, an English teacher, shows the seamless relation between knowing oneself and knowing students and the consistency and meticulous dedication that teaching children in a personalized environment requires.

Today, my father says on the phone, "It's a good week to prune. You can actually see the buds and cut the roses so that you can direct them the way you want them to grow." He is so diligent about pruning. Every year he reads the *Farmer's Almanac* and gardens according to its recommendations. Years of experience have given him a green thumb. Plants and trees thrive under my father's care. I listen carefully to his words and can't wait to get started on pruning my own roses in my backyard. Every year he goes to my tia's house and prunes her vines and trees. He knows what he is doing and every year the trees yield *so* much fruit: grapes, peaches, and loquats.

It's a chilly Saturday morning in January and the misty fog is still lingering over the Gavilan hills. I get my gardening gear together and go out back. As I am pruning, I think of my father's words and how knowledgeable he is about gardening. He is always so consistent. The cold nips at my hands and oftentimes the wind makes me contemplate staying inside and enjoying another cup of coffee. However, with each snip, I feel a sense of accomplishment, and in the back of my mind I have hopes of enjoying the beautiful flowers in the summer. I think of my students.

Just as my father has become a better gardener, I too have become a better teacher over time. All of my experience and education has allowed me to guide my students on more successful paths. Antonio came into my English classroom barely writing a coherent paragraph. After migrating between the United States and Mexico for several years, his family has opted to stay here for most of the school year.

The school focus on writing has had a tremendous impact on my teaching. On the district writing tests, Antonio jumped from a failing score up two levels to a passing score. Because of a focus on research and using data to make better decisions about how to get at increasing student achievement, I am able to track his progress and tailor my teaching to his academic needs and goals. Surely, many things can be attributed to his academic improvement, but simply looking at Antonio's work in English from the beginning of the school year to this spring, one can see significant growth. Often I have encouraged him to complete his work and be prepared for class. He was placed in an appropriate reading group during class time to meet his reading level needs. He has received individualized instruction. He has also been given a lot of feedback about his writing and encouragement to continue to work hard academically. Last, he has stepped up to the challenge of getting the most out of his education by working hard and asking for help.

Many students in this Specially Designed Academic Instruction in English (SDAIE) class have become better students. During this school year, reading the autobiographical book, *The Circuit*, by Francisco Jimenez, was such an empowering experience for this class. Many of the students, especially Antonio and another student, Sophia, related to the main characters' difficult and rewarding experiences of learning English. Sophia, whose aunt had introduced her to the book the previous year, was quite excited about a trip to Santa Clara University that I had scheduled to meet the author.

During our class exercises of writing Jimenez a letter, she wrote two pages' worth of commentary and questions. She even asked him questions in person, got his autograph, took his picture, and stayed after until she was the last student to leave for the lunch break. "You, too, can come to school here!" Jimenez told her, and she beamed. I was so proud to see her interacting with this author and see her realize the enormous potential that she has in front of her. Her eagerness to do well in education is so similar to that of Jimenez and many English language learners who see the myriad possibilities in this country.

In the last two years, I feel I am getting a better sense of what it means to advocate for all students. Simply by choosing to continue to teach English Language Learners (ELL) instead of just focusing on AP classes, I can make a difference in the quality of education that ELL students receive at my site.

I do a lot more this year in terms of assessment and making curriculum decisions based on data. Some of the positive steps that I have taken over the last two years are sharing district reading scores with students, holding individual writing conferences and goal setting with students, giving better feedback on writing by using the "Six plus One" trait scoring rubric for planning curriculum (developed by McTighe and Wiggins, 2004, in their book *Understanding by Design*), participating on a districtwide ELL task force, and becoming the English Department chair. The combination of these activities makes my classroom, this school, and this district a place where rigor and high expectations in academics is the norm for all students.

My mind recalls another spring day when my father helped me and my two siblings plant three redwoods in our front yard. Years later, when I visit my childhood home, these trees stand tall and resilient. Knowing that they started with some direction has given me a sense of hope about life and the extra encouragement that we all need. Little did my dad know that he was not only nurturing a gardener in me, but he was creating a patient student and teacher leader. Being outdoors and seeing plants grow has taken on a whole new meaning.

I prune another branch. The small bud can be seen below, pushing out, despite the cold weather lately. Another branch actually has a small orange flower, somehow protected by other branches. The rose is fragrant and held up by a deep red stem. It has grown late into the winter, despite the frost. It is motivated to grow, and with just a bit more time it could have been even stronger. I look around and see other buds that are present and waiting. They need a little more care and guidance. The spring awaits, and so do many other seasons.

Reflective Questions

- Ms. Diaz's pruning metaphor leads us to understand her as a caring and effective teacher. How does this metaphor apply to her own learning? What metaphor works well for you?
- What would you say is similar between Antonio's and Sophia's school experience?
- How does Ms. Diaz interact with the rest of the staff?
- How many teachers like Ms. Diaz do you know at your site?

STUDENTS' ACADEMIC PERFORMANCE AT THE CENTER OF STAFF CONVERSATIONS

Mary Beth Boyle, a literacy coach for her school district, captures how coaching her colleagues to address the tensions and dilemmas they confront—for instance, around assumed knowledge and understandings of students' cultural backgrounds—challenged her own assumptions.

Knowing how and when to nudge someone gently down a rocky path and knowing when to push back hard and furiously is a delicate act. In the last two years, through my work as a new teacher advisor, I have focused much of my energy on helping teachers become aware of, gather data about, and learn strategies to address the inequities in their schools and classrooms. This work has involved a great deal of pulling and pushing at times, even within me.

Last year, I worked with a new teacher who asked me to help him figure out what was wrong in a class where he felt the students were always challenging his authority. I observed in his classroom a number of times, and I became aware of some patterns that I wanted to help him see and change. The class had a large number of Latino students, mostly male, and three young White women who dominated class discussions and were vocal about their dissatisfaction with the class. I began collecting data for him about the interactions I observed between and among his students and him. I used a tool that I had learned about the previous summer at Enid Lee's Equity Institute, which was designed to help teachers "check their equity systems" (see this chapter's Resources section). The questions help to prompt teachers to reflect on their practices, and I was using the prompts and the data to help this particular teacher look for patterns as to who was speaking in his class (and who was not), as well as what comments he was making and to which students. There were many inequities in the ways he interacted with students that he was unaware of, and through the data I was trying to bring these issues to light.

That same year I was working with a fifth grade teacher who shared with me in conversation her plan to do a simulation at the beginning of her social studies unit on slavery. Her idea was to strew the floor of the classroom with cotton balls and have the students pick them all up. Her intent was to give students an opportunity to build empathy with slaves for the backbreaking work of cotton picking. She had two African American students in her class; and after acknowledging the intent of the activity, I was able to engage her in a discussion about what it might mean to a Black child to participate in this activity versus a White child. She had not thought of it in these terms, and after some conversation we came up with some different activities intended to build students' empathy and critical thinking that were more respectful of students' cultures and backgrounds.

My role provided me with an opportunity to influence a wider band of classrooms when I worked with the administration to create a professional development opportunity for a group of new and veteran English and social science teachers. As part of a ninth grade Global Studies course, this group of teachers was about to begin a unit on Africa. As I engaged in conversations with the teachers, most of whom had little background knowledge or formal study of the vast continent of Africa, I formulated a plan. Through my work with Enid Lee, I had met Clem Marshall, a scholar who has devoted much of his adult life to the study of Africa. With the support of the principal, I was able to secure four release days for these six teachers to jointly develop and refine their Africa unit. With Clem's help, we read and learned together and developed a unit much farther along the continuum from a contributions approach to more of a transformation approach.[1]

I think what we accomplished over these four days was only a first step, but an important one. We put race on the table for discussion, as Enid says. We struggled with and were honest about beginning to explore our own biases and lack of knowledge about a whole continent and its people. We had intense discussions about a map that Clem shared that put Africa at the center of the world. We created an activity for students to explore their own knowledge base, misconceptions, and biases about Africa by having them generate lists of words and images that they associated with Africa and then to try to trace where those particular images originated for them.

These four days were powerful ones and reflected professional development at its very best—relevant, collaborative, responsive to teachers' needs and development, and invigorating. We pushed against biases within ourselves and represented in the textbook and were pulled along by our desire to expand our students' experiences and not perpetuate these biases.

Even in the current educational and political climate with its emphases on basic skills and test scores, it is critical that we remember the role that education can play in creating not only a more literate world but a more just one as well.

Reflective Questions

- What would you say are the thematic threads of Ms. Boyle's work with these teachers?
- What does race have to do with equity?
- How about social class and gender?
- How do you think Ms. Boyle's approach helped children's academic performance?

HAVING THE EQUITY CONVERSATION

Monitoring students' academic performance and identifying the teachers and their practices that make high performance possible requires the critical and active eye of teacher leaders. As transformative agents, they usually encounter silent resistance and, at times, outright and open opposition from staff who are either unaccustomed to monitoring student performance or not imbued with the habit of reflecting on their own practices, or both. Teacher leaders rely on data as the most important point of departure for breaking with these traditions.

115

Teacher leaders who closely tie their work to a position of equity of opportunity and outcomes search for the documented evidence showing how well students are performing. Identifying who specifically performs well and who faces challenges among the different social groups is not a casual endeavor; it is built as a routine in the school's schedule. Following up on pedagogical practices and classroom delivery methods that produce the best results is not an informal and haphazard task; it is purposefully organized, and a commitment to doing so shapes the way things are done. In other words, these two activities constitute a habit and form part of a culture anchored on the belief that all students must have equitable access and produce equitably.

Marc Davis, an elementary school teacher, tells how he engaged his colleagues and used the resources available to initiate a cultural shift at his school. Mr. Davis sought to connect the school's focus on equity outcomes to daily talk.

Barrett Elementary is a newly constructed school located in a city of just over 33,000 residents. The school is surrounded by both new high-income housing tracts and low-income housing projects. The student population consists of 485 students in Grades K–6 from 19 different ethnic groups and is predominantly white and Latino. While each teacher constantly assesses student progress through conferencing and observations, no norm- or criterion-referenced data are collected. Student work is assessed using rubrics generated in class. However, the rigor and content of rubrics vary from classroom to classroom. Workshop-based literacy instruction has motivated teachers and students but does not include any uniform means of assessing student performance in reading.

At all the school district elementary schools, reading assessment data (i.e., running records) are required from all elementary teachers three times during the school year. Results from the running records in each classroom are submitted to principals, who forward them to the district office. Elementary principals also keep reading assessment results on file in the school office. State standardized reading test scores are kept with student cumulative files and in a binder in the school office. Scores from state standardized tests are not presented to teachers until the following school year.

The running record data (specifically decoding and comprehension scores) submitted by teachers are not used to determine the needs of low-performing student populations *across* grade levels. Running record data are used to guide classroom instruction, but teachers are only aware of the literacy progress of students in their own individualized classrooms.

When discussing possible reading interventions for students at staff meetings during the 2002–2003 school year, the staff and school administration felt that an afterschool literacy program should only be offered to students who were performing slightly below grade level in reading. The staff often decides to focus on students with the most potential for growth in reading. Interventions for students performing far below grade level in reading were not considered.

Afterschool reading interventions—six weeks of small guided reading groups—were offered two consecutive years, and students were grouped by running record scores within each grade level. However, no data were collected during or after the interventions. Students were simply exited from the intervention at the end of the six-week period without any plan for communicating a student's progress. Therefore, the staff had no evidence that the interventions were effective or even designed properly.

Despite the lack of data collection and analysis for the intervention, it was offered again during the following school year; nor were data collected before or after the intervention this time. During the 2003–2004 school year, support for the intervention had fallen, and not enough teachers were willing to continue the program. Despite the availability of data, I realized that we lacked a culture of teachers empowered to use data to drive instruction.

I then studied what teachers already knew about data analysis tools and what they needed to know to support instruction with data. A data analysis tool called the "Assessment Wall" was used to present data to teachers in a simple visual format.

The Work

An Assessment Wall tracks academic progress using charts displayed in a large table that contains every single student's name by grade level. Each student is represented with a colored Post-It note labeled with various information and data. Colleagues from a neighboring school district who taught me this technique used the Assessment Wall charts to ensure that each child was progressing, and those behind grade level expectations were immediately placed in an appropriate group.

After presenting the Assessment Wall concept to my principal, I determined that enough data sources were available—although our school was only in its second year of operation at full capacity—for our staff to track student progress.

Basic student information such as names, age, gender, and grade level were obtained from our school attendance clerk, who printed class lists using the school's attendance software. Because our school did not have a list of English Language Development (ELD) students and their language test scores, our English as a second language (ESL) paraprofessional highlighted the names of ELD students and noted their ELD levels by hand. Running record scores, reading intervention records, retention records, and standardized test scores were obtained from files kept in the principal's office. Other information such as speech and counseling enrollment had to be found by consulting the representative for each program at the school. All collected data were entered into Microsoft Excel spreadsheets and presented to teachers.

At first, the Assessment Wall was offered to the staff as a way to better understand California standardized test scores and apply them to instructional practices. But by the winter of 2003, we began discussing the Assessment Wall as a means to help teachers regularly use data and track student progress over time. The principal provided two staff meetings, a few months apart, to revisit the Assessment Wall and guide the staff to see a need for carefully developed reading interventions.

I conducted two teacher surveys. The first was given to teachers at the beginning of the intervention. This survey was designed to show what kinds of data teachers used, when they used data, and how comfortable they felt examining different types of student performance data. Teachers reported a wide range of comfort levels analyzing statewide standardized test data. Some teachers seemed comfortable using state test data because they were taught to analyze them at previous schools or in previous districts. Others felt uncomfortable interpreting data from a class they no longer taught.

Teachers appeared to have been habituated to doing two concurrent activities: (1) they were using student work to drive their classroom instruction and (2) they were not disaggregating data in their performance analysis. Both of these practices were critical to using data to drive instruction. Teachers were ready to begin looking at student performance data as a whole school, tracking individual student and student cohort progress. However, teachers still needed a tool allowing them to utilize state test scores to enhance instruction.

At the first Assessment Wall session, teachers were introduced to the concept of the Assessment Wall and trained to create student profile cards. Student profile cards consisted of large colored Post-It notes—which represented a student's ethnicity—with a student's name at the top, along with colored adhesive dots on each card. The colored dots represented variables such as reading level, ethnicity, special needs, Gates-MacGinitie score, and so forth.

Teachers were given 30 minutes to assemble student profile cards for their class and post them on a grade level chart. The grade level charts were divided into four columns representing the possible quartiles for SAT/9 total reading scores. Teachers were then directed to discuss the patterns visible on their grade level's Assessment Wall chart for 15 minutes. At the end of the 15 minutes, teachers shared observations with the whole staff. Designed as an introduction to the Assessment Wall data analysis tool, teachers were not prompted to act upon patterns of inequity at this first meeting.

The second survey was given to teachers after the first presentation of the Assessment Wall. In order to generate a stronger interest in the flexibility of the Assessment Wall to disaggregate diverse types of data, teachers were instructed to circle three kinds of possible data sources they wanted to know more about from a given list of twelve sources. Space was provided for teachers to write down any sources of data not represented in the list. Survey data helped determine how teachers felt about data use practices and what knowledge they wanted to gain from analyzing student data. The information collected in this and the previous survey was used to plan subsequent presentations of the Assessment Wall.

At the second session, teachers created Assessment Wall charts for the school year. This time, fewer variables were included on each student profile card. Teachers were able to assemble the new Assessment Wall in 15 minutes and then spend 30 minutes discussing patterns in grade level teams. After this session, teachers were surveyed on the kinds of data they wanted to place on student profile cards for the next session. Most teachers wanted to see attendance, language test scores, and student mobility represented on the Assessment Wall. However, the principal and I determined that the staff might need more instruction about the purpose of the Assessment Wall (to use data for the meaningful improvement of student achievement); there was no consensus among teachers about which variables to examine to determine student reading progress.

At the third session, teachers compared two years' Assessment Wall charts. Teachers sat in grade level teams and used an open-ended questionnaire to guide their discussions about trends in student data over time. After grade level discussions, the staff regrouped and shared key points from their conversations. The staff also decided to reassess the three types of data they wanted to add to the Assessment Wall.

Results

Analyzing the Assessment Wall, teachers noticed that English Language Learner (ELL) students had not progressed significantly between the 2002–2003 and 2003–2004 school years. Teachers agreed that interventions were necessary in order to raise students out of the bottom two quintiles in the state's standardized test total reading scores. By identifying the student population that needed immediate intervention (ELL students), teachers were using data previously ignored or used only in isolation.

As the staff began to familiarize themselves with data analysis techniques and internalize the need for evidence, critical changes in attitudes began to occur at faculty meetings. The patterns in student achievement and failure on the Assessment Wall charts were undeniable, and teachers began to understand needs among large populations, not just their own classes. It quickly became clear that interventions for failing students were needed and that patterns of failure would not improve without action.

Rather than require teachers to use advanced statistical techniques, the Assessment Wall presented data to teachers in a useful, palatable form. By empowering teachers to improve school practices using inquiry and frequent assessments, our school kept student success at the center of change.

Reflective Questions

- What characterized the direction of instruction at Mr. Davis's school prior to using the Assessment Wall?
- How different was the school's culture after using the Assessment Wall?

- If it is true that a cultural shift is taking place at Barrett school, what would you say are its key features? If not, why do you think a cultural shift is not happening?
- How can you use Mr. Davis's approach to support a data dialogue at your site?

WHAT EQUITY-FOCUSED SCHOOLS LOOK LIKE

As we have shown through the narratives of teacher leaders above, successful schools exhibit an ethos made up of three key factors: (a) leaders distribute resources targeting students' challenges and needs, (b) leaders strive to fully personalize students' learning, and (c) leaders focus staff conversation on equity outcomes. Obviously, school leaders working with a clear and unambiguous focus on equity is the precondition for these three factors to exist. Virginia Frazier-Maiwald tells how Edenvale Elementary embodies some of these factors. This story shows what a school working to increase learning for all students looks like.

Academic Success

Edenvale's population consists of 92% students of color, 68% English Language Learners, 20% mobility rate, and 78% students on free or reduced-price lunch. The first two hours of the day are considered "sacred time," and instruction is uninterrupted. Everyone provides literacy instruction at the beginning of the day. This activity makes it possible for teachers to create student reading and writing groups at various skill levels. Thus, teachers focus more intensely on teaching a narrower range of skills. Flexible grouping of students and departmentalization, based on the teacher's professional strengths and interests, helps to decrease time pressures, especially when the school attempts to organize learning experiences in each curricular area for *all* students.

The school provides teachers with four grade level team-planning days during the school year (substitutes provided) for collaboration and sharing of effective instructional practices. Teachers map the curriculum, helping this way to ensure that classroom learning activities are aligned with state standards and assessments. Through the mapping process, teachers are able to see where the gaps exist in the school's instructional program and also identify the overlap of academic concepts.

The curriculum materials mirror the student population, including their variety of cultures and life experiences. Instruction is organized around cooperative learning, a variety of sheltered teaching strategies, and appropriate English language development support. Students in fifth and sixth grades complete projects on their family's cultural background, and parents come to the classroom to share their family and place-of-origin traditions, dress, food, and stories. In addition, technology forms an integral part of the school's curriculum. For instance, every child participates in the Accelerated Reader Program, and students conduct their research through the Internet and complete multimedia projects. In the fifth and sixth grade, they learn how to use PowerPoint for classroom presentations.

High Expectations

Juwan races to school. He must get in the breakfast line early to be ready for the school year's first Adopt-A-College program assembly. For over a decade, students have experienced this ritual. Juwan excitedly awaits his presentation at the assembly. His class has written a rap about going to college, and they will perform it at the event. He knows that he must remember his lines perfectly. This is Juwan's favorite day of the school year. He will meet his college pen pal as well as former Edenvale students now in college. Juwan watches how his tearful teacher greets the former students. They are present to tell their college stories and the importance of working hard during the elementary school years.

The college students remind Juwan about the importance of doing his personal best, an important behavioral guideline at the school. Some of the former students have traveled far to join in this college day event. On this day, everyone wears a college shirt provided by donations from colleges across the country. Juwan has visited San Jose State University where his pen pal attends college. His pen pal has written to answer all of his questions about that university campus.

The assembly begins and his class takes the stage. The audience begins clapping along with the rap and begins to follow the lyrics.

The energy in the cafeteria grows, and soon everyone is absorbed in this day's Adopt-A-College assembly. Juwan stands at the front of the stage and delivers his lines. Everyone applauds.

The whole audience joins in the song to the tune of "Johnny B. Goode." It speaks of hard work and perseverance. Juwan replaces the word *Johnny* with his own name and hums the tune throughout the day. The family's small apartment echoes with Juwan's version of the school's new song. His little sister imitates his singing, and Juwan speaks to her about going to college. Juwan has obviously absorbed the message about college and talks to his family about his plan. As Juwan reluctantly takes off his college T-shirt at the end of the day, he definitely seems to know in his heart that he wants a college education to be a part of his future. These elementary school students write to college buddies, participate in special assemblies, and visit college campuses. They are beginning to integrate a personal expectation that college is a part of their future. When this program began 15 years ago, 27% of the students from this school went on to college. This fall, 85% were accepted to colleges and universities throughout the country. This culture emanates a heartfelt theme that our students will be successful learners.

Culture of Evidence

How can instructional staff effectively monitor student progress? How do we know which students are successful and which require additional support? The school district adopted a practice known as the "Assessment Wall." Every elementary school within the district is committed to list the reading and writing levels of all students by classroom teacher. Each teacher prepared a record of student progress on large sheets of butcher paper. Statewide standardized test results, along with quarterly and monthly benchmarks (Gates-MacGinitie score, running records, and writing assessments), identify which students begin the year below grade level standards and the degree of student progress during the year in reading and writing skills. Race, ethnicity, gender, and language status are identified to provide disaggregated data. Assessment Walls provide useful data for grade level and schoolwide meetings. One indication of success might be the school's ranking by the California's Academic Performance Index (API) that compares similar schools. The school's API has lately increased over 85 points.

The instructional staff assembles to create the Assessment Walls. A colorful scrap of paper represents each child and his or her gender, ethnicity, and unique learning needs. The teaching team is clear on where to focus and how to more effectively collaborate in order to facilitate student success. Each grade level's Assessment Walls are hung in the Professional Development Room. The sheets of butcher paper are then posted in chronological order from kindergarten through sixth grade around the room. Each teacher examines every grade level chart and looks for schoolwide achievement patterns. Deficiencies in student performance are recognized, and points of intervention for these deficiencies are addressed. The information in this room is confidential. The Professional Development Room is kept exclusively for teachers to analyze, reflect, and discuss a variety of data regarding student academic progress.

Personalization

Cruising her room, Ms. Hernandez, a young Latina educator who actually grew up in a neighborhood close by, was warmly greeting her students. Leticia, now in third grade, thinks that Ms. Hernandez is the most beautiful teacher she has ever seen, and she also knows that she is very strict. The students had heard that by the end of the first day of school they would have to recite the school's behavioral guidelines. While Ms. Hernandez is known in the community as a no-nonsense "enforcer of the Edenvale way," her students are secure in her classroom as she consistently demonstrates a balance of warmth and affection with discipline.

Leticia remembered how difficult school had been last year when she was in second grade. In the middle of the year, a new teacher showed up, and the child never saw Ms. Moore again. Leticia often walked home after school with tears streaming down her cheeks, spent most of that year filling out worksheets that she did not understand, and looked down at the floor when the teacher posed a question to the class. The classroom seemed tense and chaotic. Leticia tells how she avoided being chosen to speak in class, as she recalled the look on the substitute's face, a signal of displeasure, which to the girl appeared to mean that her English was not very good.

Fortunately, Ms. Hernandez's teaching suggests that she is cognizant of this child's strengths and challenges, since the academic program has been carefully designed to engage her more fully with literacy development. Leticia participates in small groups where she will very likely feel more comfortable participating in class. Ms. Hernandez has chosen her as a "focal student" and has committed to working with her twice a day and to focus on reading and writing skills. Transitional reading strategies and sheltered English instruction, as well as the use of the primary language, are some of the scaffolding strategies the teacher will use to fortify this student's reading skills. Ms. Hernandez will closely monitor the girl's progress, ensuring that she moves into the "proficient" quintile, as measured on standardized testing in the spring. Leticia has a beautiful voice, can sing in Spanish and English, and loves to perform with the school's Folkloric Dance Club. Ms. Hernandez knows this student's talents, and she too loves folkloric dance, having considerable performance experience herself.

Ms. Hernandez incorporates Leticia's dancing into lessons; for instance, she begins the first math lesson of the year by using a word problem involving the counting patterns in the "Lingo Lingo," Leticia's favorite dance, to reinforce multiplication. The child's face glows with satisfaction and gazes with affection at her teacher after realizing that Ms. Hernandez had chosen her especially for this first example. Leticia appears to feel better about her mathematics ability. Her teacher has begun her work targeting Leticia as a focal student and connecting her to a higher level of academic success and meaningful engagement with school.

Leticia races home from school this very first day with a special note from Ms. Hernandez. The note was discussed with her so that she will be able to communicate about it with her grandmother. The student is supposed to go to Homework Center daily after school for personal tutoring and homework support. Leticia is excited at the prospect of staying after school with her teacher. The child will very likely be paired with a special upper grade buddy. The teacher plays the same kind of music Leticia's grandmother listens to. This classroom is a sanctuary for the child. Her teacher too is now a role model who links her interests to the school and the formal curriculum in a way that seems meaningful. A bridge has been erected. Leticia is no longer concerned that her family does not read or write English. Her teacher understands.

The grandmother is personally invited to attend English as a Second Language class at school. Though this is unfamiliar territory, she seems comfortable talking with Ms. Hernandez and gives it a try. She finds her neighbors as well as dozens of other students' relatives at the school. The best part was meeting some people in the class who are immigrants from a neighboring village in Mexico.

Now she attends classes three days a week. She has become comfortable at the school and helps the teachers in other ways. This relationship adds to Leticia's bond with Ms. Hernandez. For the first time, Leticia is experiencing a feeling of high status as a learner.

Networking

During the last five years, the district has had as a major focus, an initiative to "Close the Achievement Gap." Disaggregated student performance data informed district leaders that Latino and African American students were underachieving. Then school personnel, students, and parents created a comprehensive document outlining a vision of expected skills, attitudes, and behaviors needed to increase academic performance by Latino and African American students.

The Close the Achievement Gap initiative provides Latino and African American parents increased access and an active voice in their children's education. "Koffee Klatches," involving African American parents, and meetings with Latino parents in Spanish provide opportunities for parents to learn more about their children's academic performance and also what they can do to work more closely with the schools. For many parents, this is the first time that schools have actively reached out to them.

Reflective Questions

- How would you describe the role visiting college graduates from Edenvale play in the school's life?
- In what ways did bonding help Leticia change her social status at the school?
- What are the school's key strategies to closing the achievement gap?
- What will you take from this story to your site?

APPLYING THE CONCEPTS IN YOUR WORKPLACE

1. Read the book by Kathleen Cushman (2003) and the article by Enid Lee (1996).

2. Continue and broaden the teacher reflection group. Assure norms and practices of trust so that participants can reflect on and share "specific practices that are or are not working to close the achievement gap in their classrooms and in your school."

3. Use the writings and Reflective and Essential Questions in this chapter to start conversations.

4. From numbers to names to faces. Promote the equity conversation. A good way to initiate a shift toward a focus on equity outcomes is by looking at data in the most unthreatening way possible. Use the Assessment Wall tool as a strategy:
   (a) What do you expect to accomplish with this activity?
   (b) How will you involve the staff?
   (c) How will the school administration and district support this work?
   (d) Who are your closest allies among the staff that can spearhead this effort with you?
   (e) What is the data culture at your site?
   (f) What are the comfort levels in reading and interpreting the different data instruments (e.g., standardized tests at the local and state level, performance-based assessments). We recommend a survey that uses a scale of $1 = I$ *am very uncomfortable* to $5 = I$ *am very comfortable*.
   (g) What is the frequency of data use? As in (e) above, conduct a separate survey using the same scale.
   (h) Once you have a sense of the staff's comfort levels and frequency of data use, you might want to organize actual trainings for teachers to prepare them on reading and interpreting different data instruments.
   (i) Be mindful of confidentiality issues for both teachers and students.
   (j) Reexamine Marc Davis's Assessment Wall procedures and adopt them to your specific circumstance.

(k) According to your site's size, build your Assessment Wall by grade or department, by subject matter across grades (vertical articulation), or at one grade level at a time (horizontal articulation)—or by a cluster of grades with colleagues willing to do the work with you. The whole school is the ideal Assessment Wall.

ESSENTIAL QUESTIONS

1. Why is it so important to know oneself (i.e., where we come from, where we stand) to do any work involving personalization?

2. How personalized are your daily teaching practices at your site? What makes it possible? What impairs it?

3. How can we engage the idea that linguistic diversity is a liability rather than a source of pride and cultural wealth? How does this issue relate to deficit versus assets?

4. What is the connection between the discipline of data analysis and equity outcomes?

5. What would you list as the benefits and the challenges of multigenerational experiences like the ones at Edenvale School?

RESOURCES

1. Seek technical assistance from organizations located near you. Here are some examples:
   - CACSEA's institutes on achieving excellence: www.iasbflc.org/cacsea.htm
   - The Asset Approach: www.search-institute.org
   - Californians for Justice: www.caljustice.org
   - The Institute for Democracy Education and Access IDEA at UCLA: http://justschools.gseis.ucla.edu/
   - Justice Matters: www.justicematters.org

- National Coalition for Equity in Education: http://ncee.education.ucsb.edu/

2. See "Checking My Equity Systems," developed by Enid Lee: www.enidlee.com

ENDNOTE

1. See James A. Banks (1993), Multicultural Education: Historical Development, Dimensions, and Practice in *Review of Research in Education, 19,* pp. 3–49.

CHAPTER SIX

Advocating for Students and Teachers

Enduring Understandings

- Leadership is all about maximizing student learning.
- Students are most successful in school when school leaders serve as advocates and involve the school's staff, parents, and general community in the education of all children.

Advocates are people who work together to create schools that exclude no group of children from the very best education, people who envision wonderful, high-achieving classrooms that are equitable for all students.

(Ohlsen & Jaramillo, 1999, p. 13)

ADVOCACY: ADDING VOICE TO A CRY[1]

Excellent school leaders identify advocates, create structures to support advocacy, and personally and skillfully advocate for maximizing learning for *all* students. Advocacy is an individual *and* collective responsibility. Our students need school leaders who accept this responsibility as a moral imperative. This is at the core of school leadership.

Such school leaders use the lens of fostering resiliency as a guide in their work (see Ch. 1; Benard, 1991; Krovetz, 1999). When making decisions that affect student learning—and most decisions do—one should ask the following questions:

1. Will this lead to knowing our students better?

2. Will this lead to high expectations for all students and improve our ability to support all students to meet these expectations?

3. Will this encourage student voice and participation?

And, these questions should be asked *with specific students in mind.* In the Master's in Collaborative Leadership (MACL) program at San Jose, we require that all teacher leaders interview three students on several occasions and use these students' voices as a lens when thinking about school practice.

Teacher leaders know how to function within the system, know how it works—its expectations, strengths, and limitations. They do not sit at the periphery but participate actively at the center of the system, participating at many levels. Advocacy is, therefore, second nature to teacher leaders. Day in and day out, advocating for each and all students' right to learn leads to making sure that the classroom is conducive to teaching and learning, that the curricula engage and motivate youngsters to learn, instructional strategies mirror the different needs and learning styles, and multiple assessment instruments effectively measure what students know. Advocacy also implies making sure that multiple voices are heard in the process of decision making and tangible and intangible resources are distributed to produce equitable outcomes. In short, advocacy is a habit of mind.

In this chapter, we share the writing of teacher leaders who serve as advocates. The first three examples focus on advocacy for students, including engaging parents as purposeful support for student learning. We also include examples of advocacy for teachers. If a school is going to foster resiliency for its students, it must also foster resiliency for the adults. Over the years, as a profession, we have done a poor job of advocating for our beginning teachers, and therefore many do not stay in the profession. We have also done a very inadequate job of providing quality professional development, and therefore many teachers do not value the opportunities when they are provided. There are times when teachers must advocate for their own working conditions. And there are times when teachers need to go to their community and advocate for formal school policies and practices that support student learning. The writings below address each of these areas.

ADVOCACY FOR STUDENTS

Special Needs Students

Many educators recognize the need to advocate for special needs students. The beauty of Tami Vossoughi Leese's writing is that she very clearly shares her own fears about doing so and the difficulties that arose in engaging her peers in such advocacy.

It was the end of a remarkable school year with only a month to go until summer vacation. Our resource specialist paid me a visit after school to let me know that in a couple of days I would be getting a new student with special needs. She told me that he had cerebral palsy and he walked with the aid of a walker due to limited muscle control in his legs. Then I was informed that the student had just arrived in the United States from India and was a limited English speaker.

I am embarrassed to admit my first thought was, "Why me?" My reaction was out of *fear,* fear of the unknown. Our resource specialist did her best to give me as much information as she could and tried to help make this a smooth transition for everyone involved, but the specific information about the boy was slim—just what had been communicated to her by the head of Student Services at the district office.

Since I needed to know more about cerebral palsy and what I might be contending with, I decided to be proactive. I got on the Internet and researched cerebral palsy to learn its causes and manifestations. This helped a great deal. Not only did this help me feel informed (not as fearful of the unknown), but it also helped me see the disability through a different lens.

The following day I learned a lot about my colleagues, and myself, when I briefly vented a few of my frustrations in the staff room. I think venting my worries was my unconscious way of saying, "Help!" Since support was what I was looking for, I was a bit disturbed with what I heard, "You must demand an aide," and "This is just the beginning. If you let them place him in your room, it will become common practice," and "They are taking advantage of you." I don't know why this was so shocking. I shouldn't judge others for reacting out of fear, just as I had at first.

My values and beliefs were being challenged and so was my ability to be a teacher leader. I kept hearing Marty Krovetz in the back of my mind asking, "Are you willing to be a courageous leader and lead by your convictions?" I ended up feeling a bit ashamed but also realized that I am human. Instead of dwelling on things that were out of my control, I thought of ways to learn and grow from the situation. I remembered that things worth fighting for are the hard things; that is what makes them so important. I realized that I was beginning to use a different lens, the lens of teacher as leader in how I viewed my role at school.

I decided this was an opportunity for me to lead by my convictions and be an advocate. I refocused on my vision, values, and beliefs and made certain my actions matched. I worked closely with my special education colleagues to ensure that my classroom environment was the least restrictive and that my special needs student had the necessary accommodations. Several staff members and parents were mobilized to assist the student before and after school to get him to and from transportation. Colleagues helped by having cross age peers (who spoke similar language) befriend him during recess while he adjusted to his new surroundings. Remarkably, these same peers took it upon themselves to continue to look out for him before and after school in their neighborhood. Colleagues who were once apprehensive about mainstreaming became supportive. I suggested to the special education staff and our principal that some school site staff development time be used for awareness and sensitivity training and located supportive resources and materials. I attended the student's Individual Educational Plan (IEP) meeting during the summer to give input to ensure that he would be receiving all necessary accommodations when he began school again in the fall.

Reflective Question

- Think about a special needs student whom you know well. How do you advocate for the learning of that student?

THE WHOLE CHILD

Given the pressure on educators to meet the expectations of No Child Left Behind, many school districts are using scripted instruction and telling teachers that the majority of instructional time should be spent teaching reading and math in preparation for norm-referenced testing. In addition, many school districts have developed policies to retain students who do not meet grade level expectations. Bonnie Jacobsen writes eloquently about her emotional response to these policies and how she needed to continue to advocate for the learning needs of the whole child.

I was in a whirlwind of emotions. There was a conflict between me, *the teacher leader* who knew about the theory of change and how I should be implementing new ideas and modeling for others, and me *the teacher,* the individual who could not cope with the direction of the change. Previously, I had helped to lead change efforts, but suddenly I was the one resisting. Every night I found myself crying—for my students and for me. High-stakes accountability and student retention were not consistent with my knowledge of what it takes for all students to learn.

I had always experienced the joy of teaching as my students discovered the joy of learning. Then the joy was gone from my teaching, and I could see the joy disappearing from my students. I used to inspire them with learning. Then I was threatening them with retention. I hated it and felt my soul shriveling. Was there a place for me in today's field of education?

I did manage to continue throughout the year. I couldn't give up on the students. Now more than ever, I needed to be their advocate. I instituted many "safety nets" for them, including an afterschool Math Club and time to do homework in my room after school every day. Although I did much more teacher-directed instruction, we continued to work in groups, and we always talked about multiple abilities. I was stressed doing this balancing act. I felt that I wasn't teaching to my high standards.

I had mixed emotions when we received the state test scores for our school. I was ecstatic that they had improved so much, but I have to admit that, in a way, I had hoped that we would not do well, just to prove that all the drill and test taking practice didn't help. Perhaps combining the best of both approaches led to student success.

I just couldn't teach fifth grade without an emphasis on social studies, so I moved to second grade. Even at the lower grades, there was too little time for project work. We needed to meet a multitude of state standards. As I look back on this period of time, I realize I still miss some of the ways I taught with student groups. However, I have also found that I have tightened up my instruction and have experienced improvement in student learning.

In my role as a teacher leader at school, I find I can empathize with teachers who still want to do their cutesy/favorite units and those who struggle with the hectic pace of meeting all the standards. I can give hints on how to manage the time, be more selective of extra activities, and still find joy in the day. My upper grade and primary experiences help me see the overall picture of the school. This is helpful when I help plan staff development. What I have learned as a result of being buffeted by the winds of change is that I must be resilient and look for how I can pursue my passion in spite of stormy weather.

Reflective Question

- Think about a student whom you know well. How do you advocate for the broad learning needs of that student?

Supporting Parents as Advocates for Student Learning

Research on student learning consistently demonstrates that the role of the parent is crucial. Maralissa Ratner, Marisa Janicek, Andrea Hom, and Lori Biagini-Gamble developed a structured way for parents to support many children, not just their own. This took considerable time on their part, but the payoff for students, teachers, and parents was well worth it.

The intervention for our action research consisted of one-on-one tutoring by trained parent volunteers using specific literacy intervention strategies for first and second grade students struggling to read. Twenty parents volunteered to serve as tutors, offering 15 minutes of one-on-one tutoring three times per week for 12 weeks for each targeted student. The parent volunteer always met with the same target student. Using ROLA (Reading Oral Language Assessment), each teacher identified areas for reading instruction needed by the target student. Our master's team developed literacy kits that volunteers used for the tutoring and trained the volunteers in their use. Each kit was prescriptive to each student's needs and contained hands-on activities to practice the identified reading skills. We also monitored the tutoring and evaluated the progress of the identified students. Our hope was that one-on-one tutoring with a caring adult would build reading skills and motivation for these students.

The triangulated data we collected supports the effectiveness of our intervention. All targeted students demonstrated reading growth over the four months; the average was 4.2 levels on ROLA. Interviews with the parent volunteers and teachers were very positive about the learning and motivation of the students. In addition, volunteers found the kits and the short time commitment made their commitment deeper; all teachers who were involved in this project felt that student learning and attitude toward reading improved and that the intervention did not disrupt their own classroom activities. Student interview data was also positive. Our conclusion is that parents doing one-on-one tutoring with target students works for our school. Our commitment is to continue this program and enlarge it in future years.

Reflective Questions

- How does your school engage parents as advocates for students?
- In what ways have you participated in this?
- What lessons should you learn?
- What might you do to engage parents to this end?

ADVOCACY FOR BEGINNING TEACHERS

The New Teacher Center has done extensive research around working conditions for new teachers. In *The Work-Life of Novices: School Working Conditions That Support or Inhibit New Teacher Development* (in press), Wendy Baron lists the 10 most challenging working conditions for beginning teachers. Numbers one and two are classroom condition and lack of materials and/or necessary supplies. If we are going to retain new teachers and build their sense of confidence and competence, experienced school leaders have to mentor and advocate for them. Imagine how Frieda might have tried to cope without Marney Cox's advocacy.

Frieda, a first year teacher, was hired very close to the first day of school to teach a first/second grade combination class at a school in a small district. Though this particular configuration is difficult to teach due to the broad range of student abilities, Frieda was very excited about her first teaching position . . . that is, until we put the key in the lock of her classroom and opened the door.

Everything was stacked in one corner against the wall, and we could see that "everything" wasn't much: mismatched desks and chairs, one table, a bookcase, a teacher's desk, fifth grade texts on the counter, some old computer components—and that was all. And everything was *tall* and *large,* designed for the fifth graders who had been in that classroom for many years. We unstacked the pile and arranged it as well as we could. And Frieda began to cry.

After calming her, I initiated a brainstorm of what was needed to make this room a teaching and learning place for first and second graders: smaller desks, chairs, and tables (and another table!), pocket charts, more bookshelves, grade-appropriate books and materials, a listening center, a working computer setup, and a chart stand. Given what we already had, and considering what was needed, we drew a map of the classroom as it should look for primary students.

At that point, I called the office to ask if the principal could come to room 15. The principal, who was new to the site but very experienced, arrived a few minutes later. He seemed surprised at the condition of the classroom; he had not looked at it since he had hired Frieda. We went over the list with him, showed him the map, and explained Frieda's minimum needs for beginning a successful teaching experience. After some conversation, he agreed to purchase a listening center, a pocket chart and stand, and a chart stand with pads for her classroom. He called the office for the custodian so that he could lower the desks and the table. He also had the custodian locate a bookcase and another table for Frieda's classroom and bring in some smaller chairs from the storage shed.

I next asked him about grade level appropriate materials for this classroom, since there were none. He was not sure where these might be located, so I suggested a meeting of the grade level teachers to go over what would be needed, what existed where, and what extras were available. The principal was able to arrange the meeting for the next morning.

Once the custodian finished adjusting and delivering furniture (and taking some away), Frieda and I put up backing paper and borders for the bulletin boards. The room began to make sense and take shape, and Frieda's initial excitement began to resurface.

It would be fair to say that this was not an easy year for Frieda; the initial challenge in working conditions seemed to set the tone for the remainder of the year. However, as I mentored her throughout the year, Frieda learned how to step up and advocate for herself and her students.

For other examples of advocacy for beginning teachers, see the writing by Margaret Butcher in Chapter 2 and Laurie Belanger in Chapter 5.

Reflective Questions

- What examples do you have of teacher leaders advocating for beginning teachers in a positive manner in your school district?
- In what ways have you participated in this?
- What lessons should you learn?

ADVOCACY FOR TEACHERS

Quality Professional Development

Professional development opportunities for teachers tend to be inconsistent and piecemeal. Teachers as a group do not look forward to days set aside for professional development because they know from experience that the time seldom leads to improvement in their classroom instruction or to increased student learning. In fact, we often call these opportunities "trainings"—a word better saved for how we treat animals—rather than "professional development" aimed at building the capacity of professionals. Marsha Speck and Caroll Knipe's (2005) book, *Why Can't We Get It Right?* offers very specific suggestions and tools to help make professional development effective. Fawn Myers writes how she advocated for the professional learning that she and peers needed and for the resource support to make this happen.

I've struggled with best teaching practices for both my English Language Learners (ELL) and my literacy level learners this year.

140

Paradoxically, I am the least confident I've been in many years regarding my classroom teaching but the most confident I've ever been in taking the active role of teacher leader in professional discussions. I've come to realize that I'm not the only one frustrated. As both Linda Darling-Hammond (1997) and Deborah Meier (1995) emphasize, the very structures in which we work defeat many reform efforts. After a conversation with our district literacy coach, she offered to support our work in the three-hour core. What had become clear to me as a result of reading Speck and Knipe (2000) is that all the teachers implementing this new program needed support in the form of professional development, collaboration, and classroom resources. With an understanding of what that support might look like, I confidently asked for a meeting with our director of curriculum and assessment, our principal, and the literacy coach. I requested three release days for our literacy teachers to watch Reader's Workshop in action. I asked that this be followed by professional development in the methodology and subsequent coaching, as well as the purchase of appropriate reading level books for each classroom.

I had already interviewed the director of curriculum and assessment for a class assignment, and I had worked with her on various projects throughout the years, so I knew she would be willing to support our literacy program. I knew she could help convince our administrator to spend the money to pay for subs and buy books. At the meeting, she was able to let my administrator know which funding sources he could use in order to finance the work.

Skillful leadership comes in knowing what motivates or inspires the individual, or understanding each individual's leverage points, and eventually challenging others to become their own advocates for growth through collaborative relationships.

Reflective Questions

- What examples do you have of teacher leaders advocating for quality professional development for teachers in a positive manner in your school district?
- In what ways have you participated in this?
- What lessons should you learn?

Equitable Working Conditions

Effective school leaders advocate not only for their students but also for themselves. There are times when expectations of professional educators do not match the expectations of district leadership, union leadership, and/or other teachers. Joan Martens writes about her experience in a new, poorly defined district leadership role and how she attempted to advocate for equitable working conditions. The lessons she learned will inform her advocacy efforts for the rest of her career.

One of the most difficult parts of my job as secondary literacy leader these past two years has been working in an unnegotiated position. When I realized that I had accepted a position that had been "flown," but not negotiated, I quickly contacted my union president to find out if the Federation of Teachers had filed an unfair labor practice against the district for hiring teachers into positions that not only added leadership responsibilities without a salary increase but changed working conditions that were protected by their contract.

I began with respectful e-mails. The new literacy leader positions (four district level positions and 20-some site level positions) were a mystery to my union presidents (unlike most districts, my district has an alliance between the California Federation of Teachers and the California Teachers' Association). They knew that our district data showed a desperate need to raise our students' reading and writing scores. To that end, the district had launched a reform in literacy, starting with the purchase of a very expensive package of "best practices" that relied heavily on a core of leaders to implement— via seminar, then demonstration and classroom coaching. The specifics of how all this was to be "rolled out" was still unfolding. Our union leaders questioned the time and training the district was investing into these leaders up front so that they could acquire the knowledge about reading strategies they needed and receive the training to lead their seminars. They questioned the need for a literacy leader to move from "presenter" and "demonstrator" to "facilitator" and "coach" in order to embed new strategies into the classroom teacher's experience. During this beginning phase, the literacy leaders were viewed as suspect by many teachers, who had not yet seen the impact of the professional development on student achievement and who only knew they were being asked to do something they'd never been asked to do before. To add to the confusion, when union presidents asked literacy leaders to enumerate their roles and responsibilities, they were given as many different responses as there were literacy leaders.

One reason for the reticence to negotiate on behalf of literacy leaders was that my union president had not attended the initial planning session that gave birth to this new brand of professional development. Nor had he been kept in the loop as the plans unfolded. While the other union president had attended that first meeting, she was not a regular stakeholder on the strategic planning team that moved plans into action. Because neither had been included, neither understood the big picture. Both presidents made it clear it was the classroom teacher they sided with in this new shift. After all, it was the teacher's familiar culture of professional development that was threatened; no longer would teachers be allowed to choose from a potpourri of one-shot workshops during the few days designated for staff development. Instead, they were expected to spend their weekly faculty meetings in intense professional development seminars on literacy and then allow others to observe them as they tried out what they had learned.

I became more insistent with the unions, threatening to file against them for "failure of duty to represent." On one occasion, a union president yelled at me that he did not appreciate people telling him how to do his job, that he was not about to give this his time. Because I had formerly been a union president myself, I knew I had the right to demand representation by filing against my union, but I hesitated. Should I rally the other literacy leaders to the cause? Should I try harder to convince my union presidents to take action? Could I get the district to bring this issue to the negotiations table? They had passed the buck, saying discussions over the leader positions had broken down because neither the Association nor Federation presidents had brought the issue to the table. By the end of the year, the window of opportunity had closed during which I could have filed. Ultimately, I had failed to act.

Meanwhile, various problems began to crop up. Each site principal articulated a different need for professional development in literacy to their literacy leaders. Soon, some principals began expecting their facilitators to do work formerly performed by resource specialists, providing pullout programs for their English Language Learners. Others used leaders to gather data mandated by the state or the district. A few principals expected their literacy leaders to take the administrator's place when he or she had to go off campus for meetings or to substitute for classroom teachers when the district was short on subs. Still, all expected their literacy leaders to implement the district-purchased, professional development program, training their teachers in a series of researched-based "best literacy practices."

Literacy leaders who were expected to collect and track site data were not able to spend time in classrooms with teachers. At one point, all literacy leaders were called together by the district and told in no uncertain terms they were to spend at least 70% of their time in the classroom. For many, this dictum came in conflict with the site responsibilities principals had given their leaders. It was at this point I planted a seed in the superintendent's mind to form a group that would include both district and union stakeholders for the purpose of reviewing professional development and solving conflicts at an informal level. Wheels began to turn.

At the same time that I was failing at educating the union presidents, I could not get my leader colleagues to see the need for a negotiated position. Nearly all were surprised to learn they were still part of the teachers' bargaining unit, had no sense of how their previously protected working conditions—hours, duties, calendar, and so forth—were deteriorating. Most were naive of their disparate or unfair working conditions; they simply trusted they were going to be treated well by their administrators, trusted the district would find some way to compensate them for their extra duties, "volunteered" to do professional development beyond their workday, and attended the "voluntary" meetings after school or in the evenings. Many found activism of a political nature uncomfortable. They saw lobbying for union action as antithetical to being a "professional."

During year two in my new leadership position, I began to talk more at literacy leaders' meetings about the need to define and protect our working conditions. I raised questions about compensation for extra hours and calendar days. I learned the norms and culture that existed at the elementary level and began—not militantly or critically—to articulate my viewpoint and propose possible actions as opportunities arose.

Eventually—and this took most of the second school year—site literacy leaders became aware that they were not being treated equitably, that administrators defined their leaders' duties widely and variably from site to site. They began to ask for hourly compensation when attending frequent meetings that extended beyond their contracted day. After the midyear review when the district began to outline its strategic plan for the coming year, leaders began to worry that they would be expected to work into the summer. They questioned the hours they had already put in to complete the work being piled on their shoulders. They began asking information of their union presidents. They came together with a common purpose.

Although the superintendent had called together a "Professional Development Coalition" to pursue better relations with the union in the interest of resolving problems arising from the shift in direction for professional development in our district—and they had been meeting quarterly—the working conditions of literacy leaders were no better defined. In May, the site literacy leaders, K–12, banded together for several meetings *to define their own positions,* then moved to take this job description to the negotiations team and ask the team to bargain on their behalf.

At the end of year two, the philanthropic organization backing the bulk of our district's reform had completed their three-year commitment. My own secondary literacy leader position, funded by their organization, was cut. Two years after beginning my initial political action on behalf of literacy leaders in my district, the issue is still not on the table. Several leaders have chosen to go back into the classroom, having been asked to do more than they felt reasonable or having been asked to divide their time between teaching and the coaching. It remains to be seen whether the remaining literacy leaders (smaller in number now in light of dwindling state and district budgets) continue to advocate collectively for fair working conditions and reasonable salaries commensurate with their added duties.

I have learned much about being a leader in this new position. Foremost, I learned how important it is for district and union leaders to work together in the design of professional development. The union has to be an integral part from the beginning so that problems such as those experienced in my district can be avoided. There are successful models of strategic planning that include union representatives throughout the process. There are districts that support and reward exceptional teachers who volunteer for difficult leadership assignments and can show success in significantly raising student academic achievement. One that has received national attention is in Toledo, Ohio: *TRACS: the Toledo Review and Alternative Compensation System,* which is designed (a) to reward accomplished teachers who assume additional leadership, (b) to "require participation in professional development activities where there is mutual union/management agreement on the potential for assisting teachers in gaining skills and knowledge that will lead to improved student performance," and (c) to retain teachers by rewarding excellence. I have given copies of this system to both union presidents and district administrators.

I discovered how far removed teachers were from my own belief that education, by necessity, is political. But I also failed to practice what I preach in that I did not take timely action when my contractual rights were being violated. Last, I relearned that to empower a community, one must educate them about their rights and be willing to serve as liaison between those who need to come to the table to solve a problem.

Reflective Questions

- What examples do you have of teacher leaders advocating for teachers in a positive manner in your school district?
- In what ways have you participated in this?
- What role should the teacher union play in professional development?
- What lessons should you learn from Joan's story?

POLITICAL ADVOCACY

Working to Impact Policy

There are times when skillful leadership is needed to engage the community as advocates for what is best for schooling our students. This is a new role for teacher leaders, who may practice student advocacy and occasionally teacher advocacy but are not comfortable approaching the community proactively and skillfully in order to mobilize the educational community to do what is best for students. This is particularly true when the issues are controversial. Christina Filios, Fawn Myers, and Theresa Sage write about a situation that was tearing apart their community as the district prepared to open a second high school in what had been a one high school town. The new high school did open in the fall of 2004.

This reflection concerns negative publicity and attitudes toward the opening of a new high school in a one high school, unified school district. Even though the school was deemed necessary five years ago, the new high school is still in the construction stage due to several legal entanglements with the neighboring city and residents. These delays, coupled with recent budget constraints, have exacerbated the fears of some members of our district, as well as parents and community members.

Unfortunately, the building of the second high school started on the wrong foot. What seemed to be a generous gift, a $70 million property donated to the district, became a legal quagmire as the district battled the City of San Jose for the right to build in a green-belt zone. Questioning district priorities has become the battle cry for our union as there has not been a salary increase in three years; our district has slipped to the bottom of the salary schedules in the county. The perception is that the expenses related to the opening of the new high school were being funded by teachers and classified staff.

Within this climate, several district employees have begun an active campaign to remove district leadership and thwart the efforts to open the new high school. This campaign has included numerous memos and letters deposited in teachers' boxes at the secondary sites, a barrage of negative letters to the editor in the local newspaper, and public verbal assaults on specific board members and district leaders. Many of these employees live within the community and have enlisted parents in their efforts. The information this group disseminates is biased and often faulty. Because the campaign has been so prolific, the negative sentiments regarding the new high school have increased significantly. We found their most recent "analysis" both offensive and misleading.

Our teacher leadership master's team has accepted positions at the new high school in the hopes of effecting positive reform at the secondary level. We decided to address the issue, as we felt that the unbridled publicized negativity would impede restructuring efforts at all four secondary sites.

Possible Solutions

1. We could ignore the negative public campaign and carry on our restructuring efforts, hoping that other employees, community members, and district leadership would eventually make sound decisions despite the aforementioned illogical proposals.

2. We could personally target and confront the most vocal members of the group, hoping to persuade them of our sincere research-based ideas about restructuring.

3. We could mobilize support which could include writing positive letters to the editor, presenting positive reports to the board, recruiting parental assistance, and involving the new high school staff in a positive public campaign.

The Attempted Solution

Although it is tempting to ignore the problem and continue working as we have been, we realize this would be an ineffective solution, as the negative campaign has gained momentum. Likewise, confronting individuals would be difficult, as their numbers have increased and there is not a safe environment for these conversations. It is our hope, then, to mobilize additional support. Some of our ideas include these:

- Present this case study to the new high school staff in hopes of expanding our ideas for this campaign.
- Organize small committees that write positive letters to the local newspaper on a rotating schedule. Since the negative publicity appears in each biweekly issue, it would be necessary to submit at least one letter per issue as well.
- Identify new staff members and parents who would be willing to help make presentations to the board, updating the progress of the new high school and its programs.
- Invite board members to an open house to meet the new high school staff to discuss issues regarding opening the site in the fall.

The logical first group to enlist for support is the new high school staff and parents of the incoming students. An intensive effort in writing letters and attending board meetings could become so time consuming that staff members and parents might burn out quickly and become discouraged. Thus, there is a need to delegate and rotate the work. Likewise, the hostile tone of recent letters to editor, presentations to the board, and face-to-face confrontations have caused many members of the community to become fearful of speaking out or writing to the paper. We are assuming that a team approach to these activities will ensure some sense of safety; it will be more difficult for teachers and parents to be targeted and attacked with a rotating approach.

Due to the political climate, including a board recall effort and divisiveness among board members, we feel that an open house would be an effective way to have open discussions regarding the goals and progress of the new site. As our current board meetings have often become contentious and are videotaped and played twice every weekend on a local access television channel, we are seeking a way to talk to board members away from this hostile atmosphere and in a way that allows us to have in-depth conversations, safe from "attack" from those who oppose the new high school. It will be necessary to be thoughtful about the groupings of board members because of their split voting record and because four of the members are up for recall. Also, the California state law does not allow a majority of board members to be present together outside of official meetings.

Team Growth

As we contemplated doing this assignment for our master's program, we debated writing about an issue that we had already successfully tackled. However, we decided to take our learning into our own hands, and although we have not yet presented this plan to our staff nor reflected on its actual success, we know that we cannot just remain angry. We need to act. As a team, we have grown to realize that we can trust each other to share this anger, brainstorm ideas, and construct a plan based on our learning.

Reflective Questions

- What examples do you have of teacher leaders affecting policy in a positive manner in your school district?
- In what ways have you participated in this?
- What lessons should you learn from this story?

APPLYING THE CONCEPTS IN YOUR WORKPLACE

1. Read, especially Krovetz (1999), Ohlsen and Jaramillo (1999), and Speck and Knipe (2005).

2. Facilitate a process with faculty and administration that creates norms that makes it safe to advocate for students and teachers.

3. Be an advocate.

4. If there is not currently a high-quality support system in place for beginning teachers, work to create such a system. The New Teacher Center is working with schools throughout the United States.

ESSENTIAL QUESTIONS

1. What structures are in place for courageous leaders to advocate for maximizing learning for all children?

2. What practices and belief systems obstruct such advocacy?

3. How are you working to change these practices and belief systems?

RESOURCES

Tools

There are excellent tools for designing powerful professional development in the Speck and Knipe book (2005).

Organizations

California Tomorrow offers many tools and reports that would be useful for advocacy: www.californiatomorrow.org

New Teacher Center: www.newteachercenter.org

TRACS: The Toledo Review and Alternative Compensation System: www.tft250.org/contract_highlights.htm

Resiliency

Search Institute: www.search-institute.org

E-mail Bonnie Benard: bbenard@wested.org

www.resiliency.com

ENDNOTE

1. Ohlsen and Jaramillo (1999, p. 37)

CHAPTER SEVEN

Courageous Followers and Leaders

Enduring Understandings

- Changing a school culture necessitates leaders skilled in leading and managing both change and transition.
- Courageous followership is required to improve the quality of learning in a school.

Faced with the choice between changing one's mind and proving that there is no need to do so, almost everybody gets busy on the proof.

—John Kenneth Galbraith (Bridges, 1991, p. ix)

It isn't the changes that do you in, it's the transitions. Change is not the same as transition. Change is situational: the new site, the new boss, the new team roles, the new policy. Transition is the psychological process people go through to come to terms with the new situation. Change is external, transition is internal.

(Bridges, 1991, p. 3)

153

School leaders who work to create schools that exclude no group of children from the very best education and people who envision wonderful, high-achieving classrooms that are equitable for all students need the skills to lead and manage both change and transition.

Leading change requires vision, motivation, professional development, resources, an action plan, organization, passion. *Leading transition* requires leaders who understand that change happens and that *managing transition* is based on building and strengthening trusting relationships among people working together toward a common purpose.

Bridges lists the following as the components of leading transitions:

- Identify who's losing what.
- Accept the reality and importance of the subjective losses.
- Don't be surprised by overreaction.
- Acknowledge the losses openly and sympathetically.
- Expect and accept the signs of grieving.
- Compensate for the losses.
- Give people information, and do it again and again.
- Define what's over and what isn't.
- Mark the endings.
- Treat the past with respect.
- Let people take a piece of the old way with them.
- Show how endings ensure continuity of what really matters.

Clearly, the skills needed to lead transition are different from those to lead change. Many school leaders focus on vision building and professional development but do not focus enough on building the trusting relationships needed to help others accept the endings and then transition to a new and, it is hoped, better future. In the business of the day-to-day life in schools, the time and attention needed to build and maintain relationships is frequently given short shrift. As Michael Fullan writes: "The only coherence that counts is what is in the minds and hearts of members of the organization" (2004, p. 170).

A key component of leading and managing change and transition is knowing when and how *to lead* and when and how *to follow*. Even in a leadership dense organization, where leadership roles may rotate, specific work at that moment involves some people leading and others following. Ira Chaleff (1995) presents a model that defines what it means to be a *courageous follower* and brings the follower's role into parity with the leader's role.

Three key points adapted to schools from Chaleff's writing are central:

1. Followers and leaders both orbit around the purpose; followers do not orbit around the leader. Common purpose drives the work, not the aura around a leader(s).

2. Followers are accountable for their leaders. Courageous followers know that leaders have to be effective to reach organizational goals and therefore every person has a responsibility to help make those leading at that moment more effective.

3. Courageous followership is required to improve the quality of learning in a school. *Collaborative Teacher Leadership* means that everyone is working toward the common purpose of maximizing learning for all students. Each person holds him- or herself and each other accountable for staying focused on this purpose.

In this chapter, teacher leaders write about their efforts to lead and manage change and transition and how and when to be courageous followers.

Spreading One's Wings: Lessons Learned While Becoming Leaders of Change and Transition

Even experienced teachers have to learn the skills to become strong collaborative leaders. Below, Donna Loose and Kathy Robertson reflect on the lessons they learned while spreading their wings. Their reflection offers the reader a wonderful case study about how best to lead and not lead new initiatives in a school and what the prerequisites are for implementing successful change, even a change that seemed so obvious and straightforward to them.

The procedure for lining up in the morning before school, after recess, and after lunch was an ongoing issue. In past years, students were accustomed to walking from the playground, escorted by their teacher, to the portables. The lines were disorderly and students were out of control before they reached the portable. Lots of instructional time was wasted. Students were now being directed to line up outside upper grade portables as opposed to lining up on the playground. Initially, the problem was defined as students having not been taught a procedure for how to line up outside the portables.

In alignment with the school's goal of creating and maintaining a safe, secure, learning environment, our team of four teachers decided to examine upper grade lining up procedures, as we had heard concern voiced by reliable sources and had experienced it firsthand. As a team of district support providers, we had the opportunity to observe other school sites in our district where similar lining up procedures were working well. The purpose of our involvement was to teach, model, and reinforce procedures for lining up in upper grades to facilitate being ready for learning, eliminate wasted instructional time, and introduce it as part of the school culture. Since approximately one third of the staff was new, we viewed this as an opportunity to introduce this change to a school culture in transition.

This raised some questions for consideration: Do other teachers have the same concerns or is it only us? How do we get all the upper grade teachers to buy in? What is the principal willing to do to support us? What maintenance can the district provide to support our efforts? How do we handle resisters? How do we get the kids to buy in? How do we handle kids who resist? How do we make it part of the school culture?

We thought we had arrived at a solution when we figured all we needed was our principal's approval for painting a numbered "T" on the blacktop outside our portable door where students could stand on their assigned number when lining up. Our modeling of this procedure would motivate others to join our plan, or would they?

Our desire to fix this problem outweighed the collective desire of everyone else on the staff. After all, we bought the paint, brush, and number stencils, and we just needed time to talk with the upper grade teachers and the principal. As a team, we made assumptions, prejudged the necessary steps to be taken, and rushed to fix the problem without buy-in through collaboration with our peers. It looked like a lining up problem, but we learned it was a much bigger issue. We were ready to step in and solve a problem when the problem wasn't even defined yet. We figured the staff would agree with our remedy without any input from them.

After reflecting on our failed effort to create change in the upper grade lineup procedure at Miner and reading *Managing Transitions* (Bridges, 1991) and *The Courageous Follower* (Chaleff, 1995), we arrived at some conclusions. First, the principal and staff saw our team as outsiders to the Miner culture, trying to bring change to a lineup system that was not seen as a problem to them. Secondly, we hastily arrived at a solution to *our* problem and proceeded to try to sell *our* solution to the principal, but not the issues arising as a result of a nonexistent lineup procedure for upper grade. Though not convinced of urgency, she half-heartedly agreed to our efforts to hold a meeting with upper grade teachers to discuss our perceived concern. However, because no strong relationships were yet built with the upper grade team, few teachers felt a buy-in to the meeting or the cause.

Given another opportunity and based on new understanding, we would build a relationship of trust with the principal and the upper grade staff, initiate a conversation on the issue of lineup procedure, and identify and sell the real problem of wasted instructional time. We would be explicit about how a consistent procedure for entering and exiting the classroom throughout the school builds security for students because they know what the school expects of them. This builds good culture and serves the common purpose of student safety and success. Furthermore, we would include upper grade staff in the decision-making process by valuing their input in solving the problem. By sharing the problem, not the solution, we would become allies, which gives everyone a chance to build stronger relationships. In turn, everyone is accountable for the success of the outcome.

Reflective Questions

- When have you felt excluded from a process forwarded by leaders?
- What are specific lessons you have learned when you have not been inclusive as a leader?

MANAGING TRANSITIONS: MAKING THE MOST OF CHANGE

The writing of Andrea D'Amico, Jennifer Analla, and Melissa Alatorre demonstrates how one team used *Managing Transitions* (Bridges, 1991) to engage specific colleagues in their action research project. At this time, their school was providing a written guarantee of reading success for all students by the end of second grade (roughly 1,000 days). This "No Excuses" approach was to be accomplished through a contract/partnership between the teacher, the student, and the parent. The partners agree to work together to achieve the literacy goals set according to the California English Language Development Standards. While embracing this new No Excuses approach to literacy, the school found that its English Language Learner (ELL) students in first and second grade were not meeting the California English Language Development (ELD) Standards and Guidelines.

Part of our action research project required the support of additional first and second grade teachers. We took the opportunity to utilize our learning from *Managing Transitions* (Bridges, 1991) to approach these teachers. Half of the teachers we needed to get onboard were people who were very resistant to change. We knew that their involvement in using the Waterford Early Reading Program (WERP) would mean added responsibility, require more work, and in turn cause them stress and anxiety.

In *Managing Transitions,* William Bridges writes, "You need to explain the purpose behind the new beginning clearly. You may discover that people do not have a realistic idea of where the organization really stands and what its problems are. In that case, you need to sell problems before you try to sell solutions" (1991, p. 53). Our team talked at length with our colleagues about the fact that our English Language Learners were not progressing according to ELD standards. In each of our grade levels, this was often a topic of discussion, and teachers felt it was difficult to incorporate ELD instruction into an already overloaded curricular day.

We met with two teacher colleagues who would be implementing WERP to let them know what to anticipate. In our master's class assignment we wrote, "We hope the general behavior from them will be a spirit of happiness, willingness, and energy. We anticipate positive involvement when collaborating with them." We spent a great deal of time and energy easing the anxiety of these two teachers. Because of our team's effort, these teachers have a positive attitude implementing WERP.

Over the next few months, teachers found WERP to be an excellent tool to bring English reading and speaking practice into the home through the program's take-home books and video tapes and that the daily, computer-based WERP lessons made a significant impact on their students' learning. *Gains for treatment students were larger than for control students* for all three assessment tools.

Reflective Questions

- In your experience, in what specific ways do leaders manage transitions?
- What do you need to learn to do in order to be an effective leader of transitions?

THE COURAGEOUS FOLLOWER: STANDING UP TO AND FOR OUR LEADERS

Leadership often involves challenging people to live up to their words, to close the gap between their espoused values and their actual behavior. It may mean pointing out the elephant sitting at the table at a meeting. (Heifetz & Linsky, 2004, p. 33)

Challenging one's principal can be very scary and requires planning and skill because such a conversation changes the relationship forever. Laurie Belanger, Nirmala George, Lori Gaines, and Kim Marion held such a conversation with their principal.

We returned in August to find that our principal had decided that our inservice for the year would be "Beyond Diversity" training. He would be the one to lead the training for the entire staff, and he had already purchased the video library for the course. The talk among the staff, both during and after the first day of the inservice, was mostly hostile and negative, yet it was never acknowledged by the administration. We were given a schedule for the remaining Beyond Diversity training dates.

We decided we should approach our principal with this feedback and ask him to rethink how he had presented the program to the faculty. We knew that if he did not approach the faculty differently, hostility would grow and the precious time available for professional development would be wasted.

One of our first questions to him was how the inservice topic was decided. He told us that it was the School Leadership Team (SLT) that decided the topic. Since Laurie is part of SLT and didn't remember that happening, we asked for more elaboration. In reality, the SLT had brainstormed many possible topics, including Beyond Diversity. The focus that the SLT chose was Dimensions of Learning. Unfortunately, when the principal asked for volunteers who would be willing to be trained and then train the teachers, no one volunteered. This led him to make an administrative decision; he chose Beyond Diversity.

The principal was already in the process of training the district administrators, and he decided that he would also lead the training for the teachers. He stated that while he wanted to have the teachers be part of decision making on campus, he could not be paralyzed into not making a decision if no one stepped up to the plate. He went on to say that he had a clear vision for the school and that by the end of the year, the Beyond Diversity training would prove to be useful in our main goal of narrowing the achievement gap.

We encouraged him to remind staff about our school vision and clarify for them why he decided to lead the Beyond Diversity training. It is clear that he knows where he wants to go with the inservice and how he wants to get there, but it is unclear to the staff.

We also encouraged him to use various tools to assess how each training session went in order to figure out how to approach the next one. He told us that he did invite feedback, but as we reminded him, it was a comment made at the end of the day when many people had already shut down. While he said there were a few people who did offer feedback, we told him that he may have gotten more if it had been anonymous and in written form. Many people do not feel comfortable disagreeing with the principal, face to face. He agreed that he would have a means by which he would elicit feedback from the staff during the next session.

We appreciated the opportunity to have a conversation with the principal and to share our concerns and ideas. He listened to everything we had to say and answered our questions. If he could just have these kinds of conversations with us as a staff, a lot of misgivings about his leadership and decision making would be cleared up. He needs to reiterate to the staff that he did ask for the staff to be a part of helping with professional development for the school and got no volunteers. We also need to remember and be reminded that being part of decision making at the school takes time and that though we may think we want more say, are we really willing to put in the time when it comes down to it?

Sharon Piazza's writing below clearly exemplifies how she led as a courageous follower, challenging people to live up to their words and helping them see the elephant. This clearly challenged her to plan carefully and to rely on the relationships she had developed over time. This narrative is long, but the reflection is very rich, and it is the last one!

I *am* a courageous follower, I said to myself. I *can* do this! These were thoughts that ran through my head as I entered Educational Services for our Houghton Mifflin leadership planning meeting. Everyone was there: our assistant superintendent, director of assessment, director of categorical services, and our Closing the Achievement Gap (CTAG) specialist. In the middle of the table sat a big elephant that no one but me was seeing or wanting to deal with.

As a district, we were in the process of changing our language arts textbooks. The adoption committee chose Houghton Mifflin with the understanding that our primary teachers, especially kindergarten and first grade, could still follow our literacy plan. In August, however, the words *full implementation* and *fidelity* in relation to the use of the Houghton Mifflin program was the message our assistant superintendent stated to all teachers and administrators. Many teachers were concerned with the new program's limitations and felt it contradicted what had been agreed upon by the textbook committee.

By late November, our kindergarten and first grade teachers were very angry about the word *fidelity*. At the last two meetings, many of the teacher leaders, including those completing the master's program, were giving specific feedback on the weaknesses of the program and its implementation. They didn't feel they were being heard. During the last inservice given, some teachers were so vocal that the presenters were unable to complete their presentation. Some of our district leaders saw the feedback as an attack on them.

I knew that the leaders of our district had thought carefully about how to implement the language arts textbook. Our superintendent, at the annual districtwide fall meeting, announced the problem and the basic purpose for the change. We all knew that we still had 52% of our district students below the proficient level. The purpose of the new language arts adoption was to help teachers teach to the standards more rigorously, with the hoped-for outcome that *all* of our students would be proficient.

So what was missing? Our teachers of kindergarten and first grade students had not been given a part to play, especially in the transition process itself. What were the strengths and weaknesses of the Houghton Mifflin program? Teachers had been given sanctioned opportunities to say what is working. They had taken it upon themselves to give feedback on the weaknesses of the program—and what program doesn't have them? This was the elephant no one wanted to acknowledge.

How can I effectively give input and respectfully challenge the leadership's groupthink? How can I use my own expertise to help them examine the elephant and all the options carefully before any action is taken? These were the next thoughts that raced through my mind as I sat in the November planning meeting. I began by summarizing for the group our district Houghton Mifflin history, beginning with our previous commitments to teachers that the kindergarten and first grade teachers could continue to follow the literacy plan. Next, I reminded them that the Houghton Mifflin representatives stated that the kindergarten Houghton Mifflin program was based on half-day kindergarten. Therefore, it was not as powerful as what we have had in place in our district since we had implemented full-day kindergartens for the past two years. Last, I referred to feedback given by both the Textbook Committee and the kindergarten teacher leaders—including my input—concerning the weaknesses of the program. The action I suggested was to have a separate release day for kindergarten and first grade teachers to give input and make specific recommendations for a comprehensive language arts curriculum for these specific grades. I volunteered to chair this ad hoc group and suggested our CTAG specialist be the cochair. Our director of categorical services offered funds for substitutes and the names of a few teacher leaders who were most vocal. The next task was inviting teachers to attend, while keeping in mind we wanted representation, if possible from every school, either on the kindergarten or first grade committee. We also wanted to have a diverse group; that meant considering years of service, race, and gender.

Keeping all this in mind, we made up a list, I created a flyer, and the CTAG specialist sent them out. We were worried about the dates. Because we needed at least 10 substitutes for each group, we could only get dates during the last week before winter break. In order to get vocal teacher leaders to the meetings, I personally went to their classrooms to preinvite them to the meeting, letting them know their presence and feedback was important to me and the district.

As I began to plan for the two meetings, I used my newly acquired learning from Grant Wiggins and Jay McTighe's book, *Understanding by Design* (1998). I identified the desired outcomes for the day:

- Data would be studied and analyzed to determine what is working and for whom.
- Teachers would feel they had a safe environment to air their concerns.
- Teachers would leave the meeting feeling they had been heard.
- Ideas would be gathered from which four to five recommendations would be made.

After each of the meetings, a plus/delta evaluation was completed. Both kindergarten and first grade teachers indicated that they felt heard and safe. The teachers developed five recommendations; one of the recommendations from each grade level was directly tied to data.

Reflecting back, I realized how important it was for me to have a plan when I entered the November district office planning meeting. The plan made my input an option to consider rather than an emotional outburst in defense of teachers. The plan gave our team a viable and focused way to gather legitimate input from reflective teachers concerning the weaknesses of the program and to make constructive suggestions to improve implementation.

By acting as a courageous follower, I learned that I could help our leadership team move beyond groupthink and effectively deal with the elephant. I also learned that providing a legitimate forum for teachers to vent concerns helps them to participate in the change process, turn negativity into productivity, and provide much needed feedback to our leadership team.

Reflective Questions

- Who are the courageous followers that you admire, and what do they do that you admire?
- What do you need to learn to do in order to be an effective courageous follower?

APPLYING THE CONCEPTS IN YOUR WORKPLACE

1. Read, especially the books by Bridges (1991) and Chaleff (1995).

2. Use the Bridges book as a lens to better understand how you deal with change and transition.

3. Use the Bridges book to plan how to engage peers in important leadership work. Start by purposefully engaging two peers who you think should not be hard to involve. Then engage one peer who you think will be

harder to involve. Then engage others and reflect on the lessons you learn.

4. Use the Chaleff (1995) book as a lens to better understand how you lead and manage change.

5. Use the Chaleff book to plan how to engage your supervisor more fully in important leadership work. Implement this plan and reflect on the lessons you learn.

6. This is best done collaboratively. Read collaboratively and challenge and lead your school leadership team and teacher reflection group to work with you.

ESSENTIAL QUESTIONS

1. What examples do you have of when purposeful, proactive planning led to changes that positively impacted student learning?

2. What examples do you have of when this planning was lacking, and how did the outcomes differ from when it was present?

3. In reflecting on major initiatives designed to impact student learning, what can you learn about effective strategies to manage transitions?

4. In reflecting on major initiatives designed to impact student learning, what can you learn about the roles courageous followers played?

RESOURCES

Tools

Both the Bridges book (1991) and Chaleff book (1995) offer ways to assess your organization.

Organizations

William Bridges and Associates: www.wmbridges.com

Ira Chaleff, Executive Coaching and Consulting Associates: www.exe-coach.com/ira.htm

Pacific Education Group helps educators focus on heightening their awareness of institutional racism and developing effective strategies for closing the achievement gap in their schools, including Beyond Diversity training: www.pacificeducationalgroup.com

Understanding by Design: www.ubdexchange.org

Conclusion

If you read this book and say, "I get it!" . . .

That is a start but not sufficient.

If you read this book and say, "I get it!" *and* continue professional reading suggested in this book *and* start a study group at your school, . . .

That is better but not sufficient.

If you read this book and say, "I get it!" and continue professional reading suggested in this book, start a study group at your school, *and* use the teacher narratives and Reflective and Essential Questions to guide discussions, . . .

That is a really good start but not sufficient.

If you read this book and say, "I get it!" and continue professional reading suggested in this book, start a study group at your school, use the teacher narratives and Reflective and Essential Questions to guide discussions, *and* work to start or strengthen collaborative leadership at your school, . . .

That is a really great start but not sufficient.

If you read this book and say, "I get it!" and continue professional reading suggested in this book, start a study group at your school, use the teacher narratives and Reflective and Essential Questions to guide discussions, work to start or strengthen collaborative leadership at your school, *and* distribute leadership by sharing responsibilities and roles among administrators and teachers, . . .

That is really a great start and a way to focus your school on equity outcomes, but not sufficient.

If you read this book and say, "I get it!" and continue professional reading suggested in this book, start a study group at your school, use the teacher narratives and Reflective and Essential Questions to guide discussions, work to start or strengthen collaborative leadership at your school, distribute leadership by sharing responsibilities and roles among administrators and teachers, *and* purposefully build leadership capacity on evidence-based decision making, . . .

That is really a great start and a way to focus your school on equity outcomes and a move toward a democratic institution, but not sufficient.

If you read this book and say, "I get it!" and continue professional reading suggested in this book, start a study group at your school, use the teacher narratives and Reflective and Essential Questions to guide discussions, work to start or strengthen collaborative leadership at your school, distribute leadership by sharing responsibilities and roles among administrators and teachers, purposefully build leadership capacity on evidence-based decision making, *and* focus skillful, purposeful leadership and resources on maximizing the learning of all students, *there is a good chance that your time and effort will result in improved student learning.*

And, if you involve partners as coaches and critical friends, you substantially improve the chances that your time and effort will result in improved student learning that is sustainable over time.

We want the reader to finish this book with five key points:

1. Students learn best in schools where everyone is focused as a team on maximizing the learning of all students. Leadership is all about maximizing student learning.

2. In this time of high-stakes testing and accountability, principals cannot lead this effort alone. Leadership needs to be redefined with building teacher leadership capacity at the center.

3. This redefinition has to be skillful and purposeful. Too often teachers accept the responsibility to lead without the institutional authority or professional skills, get frustrated by the lack of impact of their work, and go back to private practice in their classrooms. Teachers and administrators can learn the habits of mind and heart and skills necessary to lead this important work. Participating in meaningful adult learning is therefore crucial.

4. Partnerships carefully chosen can be a valuable component in helping to build these skills and habits of mind and heart.

5. You can lead and engage others to lead this effort!

It is our expectation that in reading the writings of the teacher leaders shared in *Collaborative Teacher Leadership,* you are inspired and hopeful that schools and districts populated by a cadre of skillful leaders are capable of achieving great things. We presented first-person teacher voices as evidence of what teacher leaders are doing to reshape the teaching profession, from redefining the meaning of leadership and the ways skills and knowledge are learned to new curriculum design methodologies. Above all, these narratives represent an example of what is possible to imagine and put into practice.

We wish that this book will provoke conversations among educators and that these fertilize hope; without hope no future exists. The teacher writings offered throughout the book are but a small attempt to capture the unbound realm of possibilities. As rich, complex, ambiguous, and dynamic as life in schools might be, one factor remains constant: our capacity to dream a better world for our children and, ultimately, our society.

Appendix: List
of Contributors

Melissa A. Alatorre is in her tenth year in education and holds the positions of Vice Principal and Bilingual/ELD Coordinator at Scott Lane Elementary School in the Santa Clara Unified School District. She serves as a Staff Developer for the district in the areas of ELD and literacy. She received her BA in Spanish and Spanish literature, BCLAD elementary teaching credential, and MEd in elementary education at U.C. Santa Barbara and MA in administration and supervision at San Jose State University.

Jennifer Analla has been in education for ten years. She is working with teachers across northern California in Guided Language Acquisition Design (Project GLAD), a program developed to help teachers effectively address the needs of English learners while still teaching state standards. Jennifer received her BA in psychology at San Jose State University and her credential and MEd at the University of California, Santa Barbara. She later went on to earn her MA in administration and supervision at San Jose State University.

Liv Barnes is in her ninth year of teaching at Campbell Middle School in Campbell, California. She has taught Grades 5, 6, and 8. She earned her BA from Chico State University and her MA and administrative credential from San Jose State University. She lived abroad in Chile for nine months, and she loves traveling around the world and outdoor activities.

Susan Bedford taught English in the San Mateo Union High School District for over thirty years serving as English Curriculum Coordinator/Developer and as a Mentor Teacher. With a colleague, she created an innovative, award-winning cross-curricular humanities course for ninth graders and loves to see this curriculum in use at other schools in the Bay Area. She has presented at many local and statewide workshops, as well as at national conferences. She now serves as an Advisor in the Beginning Teacher Support and Assessment Program and is an instructor in the teacher-training program at Notre Dame de Namur University. She relishes helping the next generation of teachers develop and hone their craft. susanrbedford@yahoo.com

Laurie Belanger has been working in education for six years as a high school science teacher. She has a BA, single subject teaching credential, and an MA in education administration from San Jose State University. lbelange@musd.org

Lori Biagini-Gamble is in her eighth year of teaching at Castlemont Elementary School in Campbell, California, where she teaches grades K–2. Lori earned her undergraduate degree from San Jose State University in recreation (therapeutic). She also received her teaching credential and MA in administration and supervision from San Jose State University through the Triple L Collaborative. Recent leadership experiences have included mentoring student teachers, participating in grant writing, and serving as Faculty Treasurer.

Lisa Blanc is in her eleventh year of teaching in the Santa Clara Unified School District. This is her second year back in the classroom teaching first grade after working for five years as a Reading Recovery teacher and Literacy Specialist. She received her BA in psychology at UC Santa Barbara, her multiple subject credential at Santa Clara University, and her masters in educational administration and teacher leadership at San Jose State University. L.blanc@sbcglobal.net.

Elidia Boddie has been teaching since 1971. She spent her first twenty years teaching Grades 4, 5, and 6. Sensing a need to make a difference for younger students, she has been teaching in the primary grades for the last fourteen years. Presently she teaches first grade at Santa Teresa School. eboddie8@yahoo.com

Mary Beth Boyle has served students and educators as a high school English teacher, new teacher Advisor, and secondary Literacy Facilitator. She has been blessed with opportunities to learn with and from outstanding students and colleagues and has served as a Teacher-Leader in the areas of curriculum development, literacy instruction, and professional development. teachermb@yahoo.com

Helena Lebedeff Bradford has been teaching high school English and Drama since 1995. She has a BA in world literature and cultural studies from University of California at Santa Cruz, a single-subject credential from Dominican College in San Rafael, and an MA in educational leadership from San Jose State University. Helena would like to write a novel someday titled *Matinee at the Drive In.* hbradford@sccs.santacruz.k12.ca.us

Margaret Butcher is an advisor of new teachers in the Gilroy Unified School District, affiliated with the Santa Cruz New Teacher Project. She received her BA in psychology from the University of California at Santa Cruz and her MA in education administration and supervision at San Jose State University. Margaret.butcher@gusd.k12.ca.us.

Marney Cox is in her eighth year of working with the Santa Cruz New Teacher Project (SCNTP) as Program Coordinator and as an Advisor to new teachers. She earned both her BA in French and her MA in educational leadership at San Jose State University. Prior to her work with the SCNTP, she taught elementary school in the Scotts Valley Unified School District and held a variety of leadership positions. marnco@santacruz.k12.ca.us

Andrea D'Amico is a third grade teacher at Scott Lane Elementary School in Santa Clara, California, and is in her ninth year of teaching. She is a Support Provider for the Santa Clara Unified School District's New Teacher Program and Literacy Liaison for her school. She serves as a Staff Developer in the areas of ELD and new teacher support. Andrea earned both her BA in liberal studies and MA in administration and supervision at San Jose State University.

Marc Davis began his teaching career in 2000 and teaches fourth grade at Barrett Elementary School in Morgan Hill, California. Marc earned his master's degree in education administration and supervision in 2004. He serves as a Teacher-Leader in his school in staff development, serves as a union Representative, and maintains the Assessment Wall data analysis tool at Barrett Elementary. His immediate professional goals include supporting other school districts in data-driven decision making and a career in school administration at the elementary or middle school level. mdavis0509@gmail.com

Katie Dequine is in her eighth year teaching physical education at Campbell Middle School. She received her MA from Azusa Pacific University, her BCLAD from National University, and her master's from San Jose State University. Katie_dequine@campbellusd.k12.ca.us

Mark DeRobertis has been teaching for nearly twenty years. He is in his fifth year of teaching at Monroe Middle School in San Jose, California. He earned his bachelors degree in art and his master's degree in education administration and supervision at San Jose State University. mmdero@comcast.net

Emily Diaz began teaching in 1996 at Gilroy High School and earned a master's degree in teacher/educational leadership in 2003 from San Jose State University. She has served as a Teacher-Leader in many areas including mentoring teachers, participating on the English Language Learners Taskforce for the Gilroy Unified School District, and serving as English Department Chair. She has also has served on San Jose State University's Leading Equity and Achievement by Design Board of Directors during 2001–2003. educatordiaz@mac.com

Joy Dvorak is in her fourth year of teaching third grade at Rod Kelley Elementary School in Gilroy, California. She earned a

BS degree in Agribusiness from Cal Poly State University, San Luis Obispo. She worked for two years in the agricultural industry before earning a multiple subject credential and MA in educational leadership from San Jose State University.joy .dvorak@gusd.k12.ca.us

Kerstin Ericsson is in her tenth year of teaching mathematics at Campbell Middle School in Campbell, California. She earned her BA in computer science at University of California at Santa Cruz and her MA in administration at San Jose State University. Kerstin_ericsson@ campbellusd.k12.ca.us

Donna Emerson has been teaching at Marshall Lane School in the Campbell School District for the past five years in second and third grades. She earned her BA at University of California Santa Cruz and her MA from San Jose State University. emerson6@earthlink.net

Tim Farrell has taught history for five years at Mountain View High School, his alma mater. He inspires kids with passion for social justice. After starting a leadership program for non-elected students who want to make a difference at our school, Tim has helped our sense of community by directing and producing biannual staff plays. In addition, he has served as a consulting teacher in the new teacher induction program. tim.farrell@mvla.net

Christina Filios is in her ninth year of teaching and is Chair of the English Department at Ann Sobrato High School in Morgan Hill, California. She earned her BA in English and MA in interdisciplinary education at Santa Clara University and her MA in administration and supervision at San Jose State University. cfilios@hotmail.com

Virginia Frazier-Maiwald is Principal of Bernal Intermediate School, formerly serving as Principal of Edenvale Elementary School. She has taught bilingual Grades K–8 and is an adjunct faculty member at San Jose State University specializing in bilingual education and multicultural education, second language acquisition, emergent literacy, and special education.

She is the coauthor of *Keys to Raising a Deaf Child* (1999) and a contributing author to *Educational Resiliency: Student, Teacher, and School Perspectives* (2004).

Barbara Friedenbach enjoys learning alongside others and has done so in many capacities during her fourteen years in education. She began as a preschool teacher and then transitioned into many other roles: Family Educator with Evenstart, first grade teacher, Reading Recovery teacher, and Literacy Specialist. For the past four years, she has coached teachers and provided site and district professional development. She received her BA in German from Santa Clara University and her MA in teacher leadership from San Jose State University.

Lori Gaines is a high school math teacher at Grace Davis High School in Modesto, California. She is in her eighth year of teaching, and this is her first year at Davis High. Her five years prior were spent at Milpitas High School in Milpitas, California, and her first two years were at Brackenridge High School in her hometown of San Antonio, Texas. Lori earned a BS in Education with a double major in math and French from Baylor University and an MA in Education (Administration and Supervision) from San Jose State University. Lori_gaines @hotmail.com

Nirmala George has been an English teacher in Milpitas High School for the past five years. She has fifteen years experience in teaching students from various backgrounds and cultures, including years in India and Canada before her assignment in California. ngeorge@musd.org

Bindi Gill is in her fifth year teaching first and second grade at Marshall Lane Elementary School in Campbell, California. She is Cochair of the second grade team and mentors college students interested in teaching. She earned her BA in liberal arts and MA in teacher leadership at San Jose State University. bindimasala@sbcglobal.net

Carlos O. Gómez, born in Chihuahua, México, and raised in San Jose, California, is a science teacher at Silver Creek High

School in East San Jose. He has been an educator for four years. He served as Academia Calmecac's science teacher for three years and as the school's Lead Teacher for two and a half years. He has a BS in biological sciences, a single subject teaching credential, and an MEd from UC Santa Barbara. He also has an MA in educational leadership and tier 1 administrative credential from San Jose State University. calili@earthlink.net, GOMEZC@esuhsd.org

Joan McMahon Gotterba is Math Department Chair at Peterson Middle School in Sunnyvale, California, and teaches seventh and eighth graders algebra and geometry. Prior to taking her present position, she taught independent study students and homeschoolers at Wilson High School in Santa Clara, California, and traditional high school math courses at Los Gatos High School. She earned her BA at the University of California Davis and her MA in education administration and supervision at San Jose State University. jgotterba@hotmail.com

Robert Hatcher has been an educator since 1977, including years as an elementary teacher and secondary math teacher. He splits his time between teaching math and being a Consulting Teacher for Santa Cruz City Schools' Peer Assistance and Review Program (PAR). rhatcher@sccs.santacruz.k12.ca.us

Andrea Hom is in her seventh year of teaching at Castlemont Elementary School in Campbell, California, where she teaches first and second grades. She earned her bachelor's degree in sociology from the University of California, Irvine. She received her teaching credential and MA in administration and supervision from San Jose State University through the Triple L Collaborative. Recent leadership experiences have included mentoring student teachers, participating in grant writing, and serving as grade level Chair. Andrea_hom@ yahoo.com

Judith Hutchison is happily teaching her seventh year at Marshall Lane Elementary in the Campbell Union School District. Over the last fourteen years, she taught in Texas,

South Carolina, Maryland, Kansas, and southern and northern California. She earned her BA in art history at San Francisco State, teaching credential at the University of South Carolina-Coastal Carolina College, and master's at San Jose State University. Judith_hutchison@campbellusd.k12.ca.us

Chris Izor is serving in the capacity of Vice Principal at Monroe Middle School. This follows teaching for four years at Monroe and completing his MA in administration and teacher leadership at San Jose State University. He continues to work closely with teachers around the implementation of Schools Attuned. cizor@campbellusd.org

Gordon Jack, an English teacher at Los Altos High School, has served for a number of years as the district BTSA (Beginning Teacher Support Assistance) Coach. He coordinates the district's new teacher induction program, guiding new teachers as they seek to master the California standards for the teaching profession. gordon.jack@mvla.net

Bonnie Jacobsen has taught for nearly thirty years in all the elementary grades. She is a teacher at Edenvale Elementary School in San Jose, California, where she serves on the leadership team. Her BA was earned in English, and her MA was in teacher leadership. Both were at San Jose State University.

Marisa Janicek is an Assistant Principal in El Segundo Union School District for the two elementary schools. This is her eighth year in elementary education. She has taught in the second, third, and fourth grades; been the Literacy Leader and Technology Coordinator; and completed an administrative internship in the Campbell Union School District. She earned her BA in liberal studies at Chico State University and MA at San Jose State University.

Steve Kahl moved to Mountain View High School from Independence High School in San Jose where he taught English and led a California partnership Academy program for students who wished to become teachers. He was already an active professional development presenter around the Bay

Area, especially noted for his expertise in differentiation of curriculum. In addition to his work with the new teacher program, he is also on the team of AVID teachers. skahl@earthlink.net

Jackie Kawashima is the Technology Curriculum Specialist for the Oak Grove School District. She is a former K–4 teacher with over twenty-five years of experience in the classroom. In Oak Grove classrooms and as a part-time instructor at Foothill Community College's Krause Center for Innovation, she works with K–4 teachers who want to enhance their standards-based curriculum with the use of technology. jkawashi@ogsd.k12.ca.us

Tami Vossoughi Leese is in her sixth year of teaching at Bowers Elementary School in Santa Clara, California. She is the Literacy Liaison (K–2) and serves on the Bowers School Site Council. She earned her BS in liberal studies at Oregon State University and MA in administration and supervision at San Jose State University. tleese@sbcglobal.net

Donna Loose is a Principal in Morgan Hill Unified School District. For two years, she served as the Literacy Coach/Staff Developer at Stipe Elementary School in Oak Grove School District facilitating professional development for Every Child A Reader and Writer Initiative. She earned her BS at Truman State University and an MA at San Jose State University. dloose@pacbell.net

Hannah MacKinnon is in her fourth year of teaching in the Social Science Department, which she chairs at Gunderson High School in San Jose, California. She received her BA in history and MA in administration and supervision at San Jose State University. Hannah_MacKinnon@sjusd.org

Kimberly Marion has been teaching in California since 1990. Prior to that, she spent fifteen years overseas as a missionary and teacher in Ecuador, Colombia, France, Nigeria, the Caribbean, and the Philippine Islands. She moved to southern California in 1988, began teaching in the Norwalk-La Mirada

School District in 1990, and remained there for four years, teaching bilingual kindergarten classes as well as Spanish and French in the middle school and high school. She has now been teaching Spanish at Milpitas High School for nine years. She recently created a common end-of-semester final exam, as well as end-of-unit authentic assessments, working collaboratively with her colleagues to create more consistency in teaching within the Foreign Language Department. KMarion@ musd.org

Joan Martens is a longtime English teacher at Gilroy High School and leader in Gilroy Unified School District. She has served as a District Literacy Coach and is an active member of the Central California Writing Project affiliated with the University of California Santa Cruz. She earned her master's degree through San Jose State University.

Nancy Migdall has taught English at Santa Cruz High School since 1980. Nancy was a Mentor Teacher for Santa Cruz City Schools between 1983 and 1998. She was a Consulting Teacher for Santa Cruz City Schools' Peer Assistance and Review Program (PAR) from 1999 to 2003. During the summer of 2003, she was the elementary summer school Principal for Santa Cruz City Schools. Someday she hopes to publish a happy novel because her students often note that most of their required reading is depressing. nmigdall@sccs.santacruz.k12.ca.us

Madeline Miraglia teaches at Mountain View High and taught previously at Berkeley High School. She brought her expertise in the Facing History and Ourselves Program and helped to pilot an interdisciplinary World Studies-English curriculum. In addition to coaching in the Beginning Teacher Support Assistance (BTSA) Program, she serves as a district Teachers Association Site Representative. madteeline.wallen@ mvla.net

Christel Morley is in her twenty-first year of teaching first and second grade at Rod Kelley School in Gilroy, California. She serves on the school Leadership Team and is the grade level Data Team Leader. She also served as a LitConn Staff

Trainer at her school, training teachers in instructional strategies for incorporating ELL students in English only classrooms. Christel earned her master's in educational leadership from San Jose State University. camorley@verizon.net

Fawn Myers, in her eighteenth year of teaching English, is working at the newly opened Ann Sobrato High School in Morgan Hill, California, with colleagues who also wish to implement change. In her role as English Language Learner Program Coordinator, she is able to raise questions about equity and engage in conversations with how to best serve English-learning students. sfmeyers@charter.net

Margarida Oliveira is in her ninth year of teaching at Rod Kelley Elementary in Gilroy, California. She earned her BA in liberal studies and her teaching credential from California State University, Sacramento. She earned her MA in administration and supervision at San Jose State University. Margarida.oliveira@gusd.k12.ca.us

Sally Peck, the Principal of an elementary school in Marin County, has been an educator for twenty-four years, including years as an elementary teacher and as Administrator. She has a BA from University of California, Davis, a multiple subject teaching credential from University of California, Santa Barbara and an MA in education administration from San Jose State University. She has been a Facilitator with Schools Attuned and All Kinds of Minds Institute since 1998. sbeugenpeck@aol.com, speck@kentfieldschools.org

Donna Peltz has been at Mountain View High School for more than ten years teaching art and has recently become an Assistant Principal, supporting students' growth through activities outside the classroom and student leadership. She has also been in charge of professional development, attendance, campus maintenance, and campus culture. donna.peltz@mvla.net

Kristin Pfotenhauer-Sharp began teaching in 1980 and became an Assistant Principal in 2003. She has served as a Teacher-Leader in many areas including curriculum design, mentoring teachers, grant writing, and school reform. She was a Board Member for the Bay Area Coalition of Equitable Schools and has facilitated workshops at the CES Fall Forum. She has also received several awards related to her years as a teach-leader including Gay Youth Ally and the California League of High Schools Region V Educator of the Year. ksharp@sccs.santacruz.k12.ca.us

Sharon Piazza has taught in the Oak Grove School District for thirty years. She has taught Grades K–5, special day classes, and been Resource Specialist, math Mentor, and district Literacy Trainer. She is the Every Child a Reader and Writer District Coach and Staff Developer. She earned both her BA and MA from San Jose State University. spiazza@ogsd.k12.ca.us

Maralissa Ratner taught first and second grades at Castlemont Elementary School in Campbell, California, for eight years. Two years ago she was a Master Teacher in collaboration with the Teacher Education Department at San Jose State University and is now teaching an ELD program for fourth and fifth graders. She received her BA from the University of Arizona and her MA from San Jose State University. ordons1@juno.com

Kathy Robertson is in her fourth year as a Professional Developer and Lead Mentor/Coach for Oak Grove School District's New Teacher Induction Program. She earned her BA in special education at Central Washington University in Ellensburg and her MA in administration and supervision at San Jose State University. Pie_gal@pacbell.net

Evelia Rosso has been an elementary school teacher for twenty years, including many years in bilingual education, and is currently teaching first grade at Rod Kelley School in Gilroy, California. An immigrant from Oaxaca, Mexico, she earned both her BA in liberal studies and her MA in education with a focus on teacher leadership at San Jose State University. eveliamrosso@netscape.net

Theresa Sage is world history teacher at Sobrato High School in Morgan Hill after having taught English and U.S. history in the middle school for nine years. She is the Cochair of the Social Studies Department and Vice President for the Morgan Hill Federation of Teachers. She received her BA in social science and MA in teacher leadership from San Jose State University.

Kathleen McCowan Sandidge graduated from UC Santa Cruz with a degree in psychology. She received her multiple subject credential and MA from San Jose State and passed the BCLAD test. She taught at Campbell Middle School for ten years, leaving the classroom to be a full-time release Mentor Teacher/ Coach for the Campbell Union School District, focusing on equity, as well as supporting the ELD teachers. kathysan didge@yahoo.com

Jennifer Schmidt is a teacher and Math Department Chair at Santa Cruz High School in California and has been a high school math teacher in both California and Massachusetts since 1996. She has a BS in mathematics with a single-subject teaching credential from California State University Bakersfield and an MA in educational leadership from San Jose State University. jschmidt@sccs.santacruz.k12.ca.us

Kelly Shannon has been teaching for fourteen years at Monroe Middle School where she teachers eighth grade science. She earned her MA from San Jose State University. kshannon@campbellusd.k12.ca.us

Melissa Sherman is in her fifth year of teaching English at Gunderson High School in San Jose, California. She is also the Cochair of the English Department and is a Leadership Advisor. Melissa earned her BA in English at Bethany College and MA in administration and supervision at San Jose State University. Melissa_Sherman@sjusd.org

Peter Stapes is in his eleventh year teaching physical educa-tion at Campbell Middle School in Campbell, California. He is the Athletic Director and Cochair of the Physical Education Department. He earned his BA in child development and his MA in teacher leadership and administration from San Jose State University.

Kristin Strand teaches second grade in West Sacramento and continues to focus on school improvement through strong leadership. She received her BA from California State University Stanislaus and her MA from San Jose State University. misstrand@charter.net

Amy Vanderbosch teaches eighth grade language arts and social studies at Campbell Middle School in Campbell, California. She also serves as the School Intervention Specialist. She earned her BA in liberal studies and MA in administration and supervision at San Jose State University. amy_vanderbosch@campbellusd.k12.ca.us

Jason Viloria is an Assistant Principal at Gunderson High School in San Jose, California. Prior to entering administration, he was a social science teacher, also at Gunderson. He received his BA in political science at University of California, Santa Barbara and MA in administration and supervision at San Jose State University. Jason_Viloria@sjusd.org

Felicia Webb is in her seventh year of teaching technology at John Muir Middle School in San Jose, California. She is also the Technology Support Group Representative at John Muir. Prior to coming to John Muir, she was a technology teacher at Gunderson High School. She earned her BA in English at UC Riverside and MA in administration and supervision at San Jose State University. Felicia_Webb@sjusd.org

Anna Williams has been teaching for seven years and is in her fifth year at Monroe Middle School. She specializes in language arts and social studies. She earned her BA in English literature and her MA at San Jose State University. Anna_williams @campbellusd.k12.ca.us

References

Arriaza, G. (2004). Making changes that stay made: School reform and community involvement. *High School Journal, 87*(4), 10–24.

Baron, W. (in press). The work-life of novices: School working conditions that support or inhibit new teacher development. In B. Achinstein & S. Athanases (Eds.), *Mentors in the making: Developing new leaders for new teachers.* New York: Teachers College Press.

Barth, R. (1990). *Improving schools from within: Teachers, parents and principals can make a difference.* San Francisco: Jossey-Bass.

Benard, B. (1991). *Fostering resiliency in kids: Protective factors in the family, school, and community.* Portland, OR: Western Center for Drug-Free Schools and Communities.

Bridges, W. (1991). *Managing transitions: Making the most of change.* New York: Addison-Wesley.

Chaleff, I. (1995). *The courageous follower: Standing up to and for our leaders.* San Francisco: Berrett-Koehler.

Conzemius, A., & O'Neill, J. (2001) *Building shared responsibility for student learning.* Alexandria, VA: ASCD.

Costa, A. L., & Kallick, B. (2000). *Assessing and reporting on habits of mind.* Alexandria, VA: ASCD.

Crowther, F., Kaagan, S. S., Ferguson, M., & Hann, L. (2002). *Developing teacher leaders: How teacher leadership enhances school success.* Thousand Oaks, CA: Corwin Press.

Cushman, K. (2003). *Fires in the bathroom. Advice for teachers from high school students.* New York: New Press.

Darling-Hammond, L. (1997). *The right to learn. A blue print for creating schools that work.* San Francisco: Jossey Bass.

Descartes, R. (1998). *Discourse on the method for conducting one's reason well and for seeking truth in the sciences* (3rd ed.). Indianapolis, IN: Hackett.

Duke, D. (1994). Drift, detachment and the need for teacher leadership. In D. Walling (Ed.), *Teachers as leaders* (pp. 255–273). Bloomington, IN: Phi Delta Kappa.

Fullan, M. (1991). *The new meaning of education change*. New York: Teachers College Press.

Fullan, M. (2000). Leadership for the twenty-first century: Breaking the bonds of dependency. In *The Jossey-Bass reader on educational leadership* (pp. 156–63). San Francisco: Jossey-Bass.

Fullan, M. (2001). *Leading in a culture of change*. San Francisco: Jossey-Bass.

Fullan, M. (2003). *The moral imperative of school leadership*. Thousand Oaks, CA: Corwin Press.

Fullan, M. (2004). *Leading in a culture of change: Personal action guide and workbook*. San Francisco: Jossey-Bass.

Gómez, C. O. (2004). Using conflict mediation as a beginning teacher support program at MACSA Academia Calmecac Charter High. Unpublished master's thesis, San Jose State University.

Goodlad, J. (1990). The occupation of teaching in schools. In J. Goodlad & R. Soder (Eds.), *The moral dimensions of teaching*. San Francisco: Jossey-Bass.

Hargreaves, A., & Fink, D. (2004). The seven principles of sustainable leadership. *Educational Leadership, 61*(7), 9–13.

Heifetz, R., & Linsky, M. (2004, April). When leadership spells danger. *Educational Leadership*, 33–37.

Hertert, L. (2003). *Narrowing the achievement gap: A review of research, policies, and issues* (ED473724). Palo Alto, CA: EdSource.

Katzenmeyer, M., & Moller, G. (1996) *Awakening the sleeping giant: Leadership development for teachers*. Thousand Oaks, CA: Corwin Press.

Katzenmeyer, M., & Moller, G. (2001). *Awakening the sleeping giant: Helping teachers develop as leaders*. Thousand Oaks, CA: Corwin Press.

Kouzes, J., & Posner, B. (2002). *The leadership challenge*. San Francisco: John Wiley.

Krovetz, M. L. (1999). *Fostering resiliency: Expecting all students to use their minds and hearts well*. Thousand Oaks, CA: Corwin Press.

Lambert, L. (1998). *Building leadership capacity in schools*. Alexandria, VA: ASCD.

Lambert, L. (2003a). *Leadership capacity for lasting school improvement*. Alexandria, VA: ASCD.

Lambert, L. (2003b). *Leadership redefined: An evocative context for teacher leadership*. Paper presented at a meeting of the National College of School Leadership, University of Nottingham, England.

Lee, E. (1996). Anti-racist education: Pulling together to close the gaps. In E. Lee, D. Menkart, & M. Okasawa-Rey (Eds.), *Beyond heroes and holidays: A practical guide to K–12 anti-racist, multicultural education and staff development* (pp. 26–34). Washington, DC: Network of Educators on the Americas.

Levine, M. (1990). *Keeping ahead in school: A student's book about learning abilities and learning disorders.* Cambridge MA: Educator's Publishing Service.

Lewis, A. C. (2002). School reform and professional development. *Phi Delta Kappan, 83*(7), 488.

Lieberman, A., & Miller, L. (1999). *Teachers: Transforming their work and their world.* New York: Teachers College Press and Alexandria, VA: ASCD.

McTighe, J., & Wiggins, G. (2004). *Understanding by design: Professional development workbook.* Alexandria, VA: ASCD.

Meier, D. (1995). *The power of their ideas.* Boston: Beacon Press.

Morley, C. L. (1994). *How to get the most out of meetings.* Alexandria, VA: ASCD.

Ohlsen, L., & Jaramillo, A. (1999). *Turning the tides on exclusion: A guide for educators and advocates for immigrant students.* Oakland, CA: California Tomorrow.

Radin, S. E. (2004). Beginning with one teacher: Inquiry at ASCEND. In A. Weinbaum, D. Allen, T. Blythe, K. Simon, S. Seidel, & C. Rubin (Eds.), *Teaching as inquiry. Asking hard questions to improve practice and student achievement* (pp. 65–79). New York: Teachers College Press.

Reeves, D. (2000). *Accountability in action: A blueprint for learning organizations.* Denver, CO: Advanced Learning Press.

Sagor, R. (2004). *The action research guidebook: A four-step process for educators and school teams.* Thousand Oaks, CA: Corwin Press.

Schmoker, M. (1996). *Results: The key to continuous school improvement.* Alexandria, VA: ASCD.

Schmoker, M. (2001). *The results fieldbook: Practical strategies from dramatically improved schools.* Alexandria, VA: ASCD.

Senge, P. (2000). Give me a lever long enough . . . and single-handed I can move the world. In *The Jossey-Bass reader on educational leadership* (ch. 2). San Francisco: Jossey-Bass.

Sizer, T. R. (1992). *Horace's school: Redesigning the American high school.* Boston: Houghton Mifflin.

Speck, M., & Knipe, C. (2000). *Why can't we get it right? Professional development in our schools.* Thousand Oaks, CA: Corwin Press.

Speck, M., & Knipe, C. (2005). *Why can't we get it right? Professional development in our schools* (2nd ed.). Thousand Oaks, CA: Corwin Press.

Spillane, J. P., Halverson, R., & Diamond, J. B. (2001, April). Investigating school leadership practice: A distributed perspective. *Educational Researcher, 23*–28.

Tyack, D. B. (1974). *The one best system. A history of American urban education.* Cambridge, MA: Harvard University Press.

Waters, T., Marzano, R, & McNulty, B. (2003). Balanced leadership: What 30 years of research tells us about the effect of leadership on student achievement. Aurora, CO: Mid-continent Regional Educational Laboratory.

Werner, E., & Smith, R. S. (1992). *Overcoming the odds: High risk children from birth to adulthood.* Ithaca, NY: Cornell University Press.

West Chester University. (2004). *An introduction to distributed leadership.* www.wcupa.edu/_information/AFA/Distlead.htm

Wiggins, G., & McTighe, J. (1998). *Understanding by design.* Alexandria, VA: ASCD.

Index

Index

Index

**CORWIN
PRESS**

The Corwin Press logo—a raven striding across an open book—represents the union of courage and learning. Corwin Press is committed to improving education for all learners by publishing books and other professional development resources for those serving the field of PreK–12 education. Byproviding practical, hands-on materials, Corwin Press continues to carry out the promise of its motto: **"Helping Educators Do Their Work Better."**